No Headache Guide to Home Repair™

I ... ir

New Century Publishing
P.O. Box 9861
Fountain Valley, CA 92708

The author, the publisher and all interested parties have used all possible care to assure that the information contained in this book is as complete and as accurate as possible. However, neither the publisher nor the author nor any interested party assumes any liability for any omissions, errors, or defects in the material, instructions or diagrams contained in this publication, and therefore are not liable for any damages including (but not limited to) personal injury, property damage or legal disputes that may result from the use of this book.

All major appliances are complex electro-mechanical devices. Personal injury or property damage may occur before, during, or after any attempt to repair an appliance. This publication is intended for individuals possessing an adequate background of technical experience. The above named parties are not responsible for an individual's judgement of his or her own technical abilities and experience, and therefore are not liable for any damages including (but not limited to) personal injury, property damage or legal disputes that may result from such judgements.

The advice and opinions offered by this publication are of a subjective nature ONLY and they are NOT to be construed as legal advice. The above named parties are not responsible for the interpretation or implementation of subjective advice and opinions, and therefore are not responsible for any damages including (but not limited to) personal injury, property damage, or legal disputes that may result from such interpretation or implementation.

The use of this publication acknowledges the understanding and acceptance of the above terms and conditions.

ACKNOWLEDGMENT

The author and the publisher wish to thank technical consultant, Dick Miller, for his expert advice and assistance in the compilation of technical information contained in this book.

©1995 Douglas Emley
Published by New Century Publishing
P.O. Box 9861
Fountain Valley, CA 92708
(714)554-2020

International Standard Book Number 1-884348-03-3

"No Headache Guide to Home Repair™" is a trademark of New Century Publishing and may be used only with publisher's permission. For information about the complete series including *Refrigerator Repair Under $40, Washing Machine Repair Under $40, Clothes Dryer Repair Under $40, Dishwasher Repair Under $40,* and future releases, call (800)392-0907.

Printed in the United States of America.

Table of Contents

CHAPTER 5: PUMP AND MOTOR PROBLEMS

CHAPTER 6: ELECTRICAL PROBLEMS

FOREWORD

WHAT THIS BOOK WILL DO FOR YOU

(and what it won't!)

This book **will** tell you how to fix the most common problems with the most common brands of domestic (household) dishwashers. (This represents 95+ percent of all repairs that the average handyman or service tech will run into.)

This book **will not** tell you how to fix your industrial or commercial or any very large dishwasher. The support and control systems for such units are usually very similar in function to those of smaller units, but vastly different in design, service and repair.

We **will** show you the easiest and/or fastest method of diagnosing and repairing your dishwasher.

We **will not** necessarily show you the absolute cheapest way of doing something. Sometimes, when the cost of a part is just a few dollars, we advocate replacing the part rather than rebuilding it. We also sometimes advocate replacement of an inexpensive part, whether it's good or bad, as a simplified method of diagnosis or as a preventive measure.

We **will** use only the simplest of tools; tools that a well-equipped home mechanic is likely to have and to know how to use, including a VOM.

We **will not** advocate your buying several hundred dollars' worth of exotic equipment or special tools, or getting advanced technical training to make a one-time repair. It will usually cost you less to have a professional perform this type of repair. Such repairs represent only a very small percentage of all needed repairs.

We **do not** discuss electrical or mechanical theories. There are already many very well-written textbooks on these subjects and most of them are not likely to be pertinent to the job at hand; fixing your dishwasher!

We **do** discuss rudimentary mechanical systems and simple electrical circuits.

We expect you to be able to look at a part and remove it if the mounting bolts and/or connections are obvious. If the mounting mechanism is complicated or hidden, or there are tricks to removing or installing something, we'll tell you about it.

You are expected to know what certain electrical and mechanical devices are, what they do in general, and how they work. For example, switches, relays, heater elements, motors, solenoids, cams, pullies, belts, radial and thrust (axial) bearings, water seals, and centrifugal blowers. If you do not know what these things do, learn them BEFORE you start working on your dishwasher.

You should know how to cut, strip, and splice wire with crimp-on connectors, wire nuts and electrical tape. You should know how to measure voltage and how to test for continuity with a VOM (Volt-Ohm Meter). If you have an ammeter, you should know how and where to measure the current in amps. If you don't know how to use these meters, there's a brief course on how to use them (for *our* purposes *only*) in Chapter 2. See sections 2-4 and 2-5 before you buy either or both of these meters.

A given procedure was only included in this book if it passed the following criteria:

1) The job is something that the average couch potato can complete in one afternoon, with no prior knowledge of the machine, with tools a normal home handyman is likely to have.

2) The parts and/or special tools required to complete the job are easily found and not too expensive.

3) The problem is a common one; occuring more frequently than just one out of a hundred machines.

Certain repairs which may cost more than $40 may be included in this book, if they pass the following criteria:

1)The cost of the repair is still far less than replacing the machine or calling a professional service technician, and

2) The repair is likely to yield a machine that will operate satisfactorily for several more years, or at least long enough to justify the cost.

In certain parts of the book, the author expresses an opinion as to whether the current value of a particular machine warrants making the repair or "scrapping" the machine. Such opinions are to be construed as opinions ONLY and they are NOT to be construed as legal advice. The decision as to whether to take a particular machine out of service depends on a number of factors that the author cannot possibly know and has no control over; therefore, the responsibility for such a decision rests solely with the person making the decision.

I'm sure that a physicist reading this book could have a lot of fun tearing it apart because of my deliberate avoidance and misuse of technical terms. However, this manual is written to simplify the material and inform the novice, not to appease the scientist.

NOTE: *The diagnosis and repair procedures in this manual do not necessarily apply to brand-new units, newly-installed units or recently relocated units. Although they may posess the problems described in this manual, dishwashers that have recently been installed or moved are subject to special considerations not taken into account in this manual for the sake of simplicity. Such special considerations include installation parameters, installation location, the possibility of manufacturing or construction defects, damage in transit, and others.*

This manual was designed to assist the novice technician in the repair of home (domestic) dishwashers that have been operating successfully for an extended period of months or years and have only recently stopped operating properly, with no major change in installation parameters or location.

HOW TO USE THIS BOOK

STEP 1: READ THE DISCLAIMERS LOCATED ON THE COPYRIGHT PAGE. This book is intended for use by people who have a bit of mechanical experience or aptitude, and just need a little coaching when it comes to appliances. If you don't fit that category, don't use this book! We're all bloomin' lawyers these days, y'know? If you break something or hurt yourself, no one is responsible but YOU; not the author, the publisher, the guy or the store who sold you this book, or anyone else. Only YOU are responsible, and just by using this book, you're agreeing to that. If you don't understand the disclaimers, get a lawyer to translate them *before* you start working.

Read the safety and repair precautions in section 2-6. These should help you avoid making too many *really* bad mistakes.

STEP 2: READ CHAPTERS 1 & 2: Everything else in this book flows from chapters 1 and 2. If you don't read them, you won't be able to properly diagnose your dishwasher.

Know what kind of dishwasher you have and basically how it works. When you go to the appliance parts dealer, have the nameplate information at hand. Have the proper tools at hand, and know how to use them.

STEP 3: FIND THE RIGHT CHAPTER according to the symptoms you're experiencing.

STEP 4: FIX THE BLOOMIN' THING! If you can, of course. If you're just too confused, or if the book recommends calling a technician for a complex operation, call one.

Chapter 1

SYSTEM BASICS
BRAND IDENTIFICATION

It seems like everyone I know has a different opinion about their dishwasher. Some seem to think that theirs is a God-send and a lifesaver; others think it's a total waste of time, hot water and electricity. Truth is, everybody's right! Within their limitations, dishwashers can provide virtually sterile dishes, if that's what you need. Poorly used and poorly maintained, they can be a huge, inefficient pain in the neck.

The main reason dishwashers exist is that they allow dishes to be washed in water much hotter than you can use when washing dishes by hand. This allows greater grease-cutting and sterilization of the dishes. They are NOT made to operate under cold water conditions or to ingest your disgusting, moldy leftovers. And using cheap soap and hard water (without making some adjustments) can shorten their lives considerably.

Wash quality is everything, and it is highly dependent on a number of different variables. Among the most important are water temperature, detergent quality, water softness, and proper loading. See Chapter 3 for an in-depth discussion about wash quality.

1-1 DESIGN AND GENERAL FUNCTIONS

The main function of a dishwasher is to cut grease and sterilize the dishes by spraying hot soapy water at them. This is accomplished using an electric motor and pump mounted at the bottom of a water reservoir, or tub. The pump takes suction from the tub and forces water up through spray arms, which spray the dishes. The water then simply drops back into the tub for recirculation.

Of course, hot water must get into the tub in the first place. An electric (solenoid) valve provides for this function. The hot water comes straight from your house's water heater, on regular house pressure.

At the end of the cycle, the water must be evacuated from the tub. The drive motor drives a pump to accomplish this function.

Even under the best of circumstances, dishwashers tend to be a little shorter-lived than other major appliances. Why? Well, to answer that question, let's all be little deviants for a moment, and design ourselves a torture chamber— for an electric motor.

What is absolutely the worst enemy of electricity in a machine? Water, right? Well, then, let's use the motor to pump water, and let's *mount* the motor right underneath the water seal. That way if the seal leaks at all, lots of hot, steamy water will run right down on top of the motor and rust it up and short it out. While we're at it, let's run some bits of broken glass and big chunks of food and nutshells and seeds through the pump, so we can chew up the seals and the impeller and also to introduce some nice, sudden deceleration shocks to the motor and pump. And of course, for maximum heat buildup, let's mount the whole motor and pump package in a tiny, cramped, steamy, dusty, poorly ventilated space, right beneath a tub full of hot steamy water. Get the picture?

1-1(a) CYCLES

Cold water can kill your wash quality. (see Chapter 3) So before letting any hot water into the tub, we must make sure the tub has no cold water left in it from the last wash. Therefore, in most designs, a new wash cycle starts with the pump operating for a minute or so in the "drain" mode.

An electric solenoid fill valve then opens to let hot water into the tub. The timer controls how long the solenoid valve stays open, which controls the water level. A flow-control washer built into the valve compensates for variations in the water supply pressure. Most designs use an anti-flood float switch to prevent accidental overflow during the fill cycle.

The pump then starts in the "wash" mode. Water is channelled to the spray

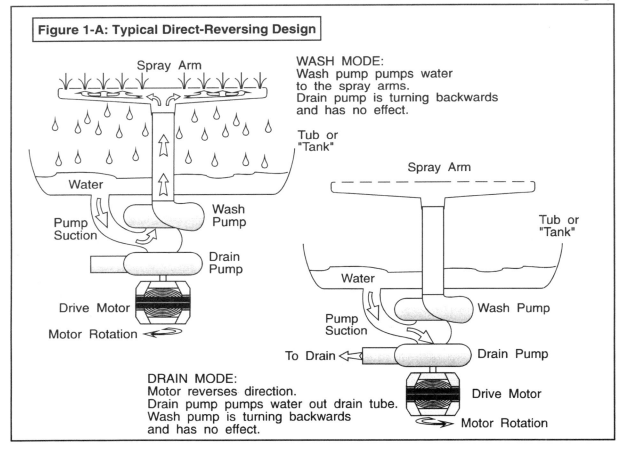

Figure 1-A: Typical Direct-Reversing Design

Spray Arm

WASH MODE:
Wash pump pumps water to the spray arms.
Drain pump is turning backwards and has no effect.

Tub or "Tank"

Water

Pump Suction

Wash Pump

Drain Pump

Drive Motor

Motor Rotation

Spray Arm

Tub or "Tank"

Water

Pump Suction

To Drain

Wash Pump

Drain Pump

Drive Motor

Motor Rotation

DRAIN MODE:
Motor reverses direction.
Drain pump pumps water out drain tube.
Wash pump is turning backwards and has no effect.

arms which spray the hot water at the dishes. In some models, detergent is dispensed during the wash cycle. The timer controls when this occurs. In most designs, the dispenser is opened either by a solenoid or by a bi-metallic trigger. GE uses a cam on the timer to trip open the dispenser.

Most designs also have a water heater in the tub to maintain proper water temperature during the wash cycle. In some designs, the heater also dries the dishes at the end of the wash.

Note that the dishwasher also operates in the "wash" mode during the "rinse" cycle. The only substantial difference is that no detergent is being released during the "rinse" cycle.

At the end of the "wash" cycle, the pump enters the "drain" mode. The pump drains water from the tub in one of two ways. In some "direct-reversing" designs, the motor reverses direction and a separate impeller pumps the water out. (Figure 1-A) In other designs, a solenoid-controlled valve opens to allow the pump to discharge to the drain line.(Figure 1-B) The timer controls the direction of the motor or the opening of the drain valve.

Most models also have a "dry" cycle. In this cycle, a blower fan circulates air inside the cabinet to evacuate steam and dry the dishes somewhat.

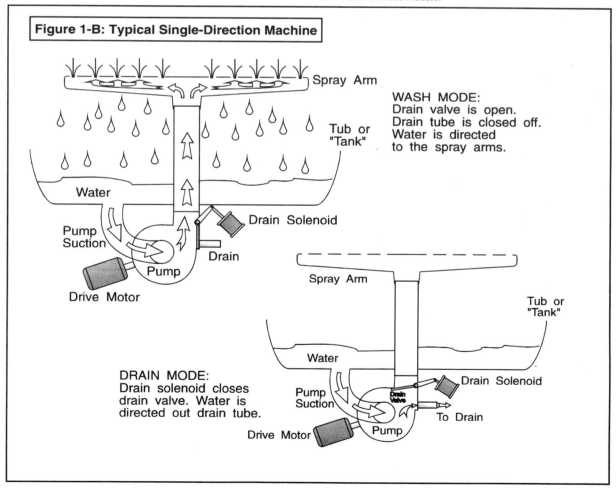

Figure 1-B: Typical Single-Direction Machine

Spray Arm

Tub or "Tank"

Water

Pump Suction

Drive Motor

Pump

Drain

Drain Solenoid

WASH MODE:
Drain valve is open.
Drain tube is closed off.
Water is directed
to the spray arms.

Spray Arm

Tub or "Tank"

Water

Pump Suction

Drive Motor

Pump

Drain Valve

Drain Solenoid

To Drain

DRAIN MODE:
Drain solenoid closes
drain valve. Water is
directed out drain tube.

1-2 CONFIGURATIONS

Dishwasher designs can be broadly classified into horizontal-shaft and vertical-shaft designs. (See Figure 1-C) Horizontal shaft machines are affectionately known as "sidewinders."

Most horizontal-shaft designs in this manual use a single-direction motor and a valve to divert the pump discharge to the drain. Late-model Whirlpool sidewinders are direct-reversing.

Except for Kitchenaid, all vertical-shaft designs in this manual are direct-reversing. Most Kitchenaid machines use a single-direction motor and a solenoid drain valve; although the latest ones resemble Whirlpool machines and are are direct-reversing.

Except for Maytag, all vertical-shaft designs in this manual have a combination pump and motor unit mounted in the bottom center of the tub. In most Maytag machines the pump unit is mounted in the center of the tub, but the motor is mounted off-center and drives the pump through a belt. (Figure

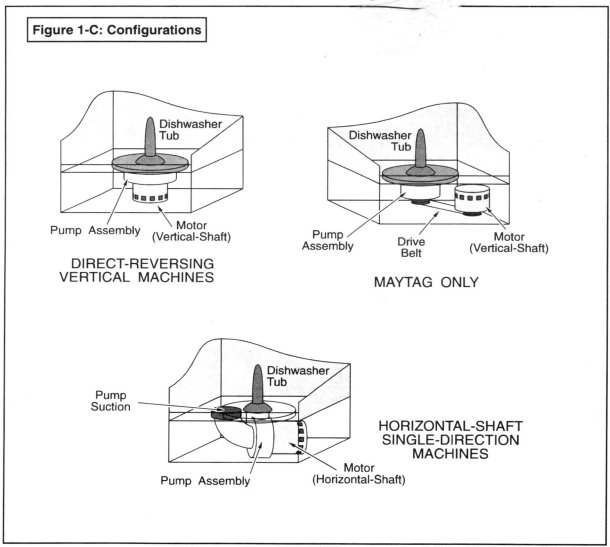

Figure 1-C: Configurations

Dishwasher Tub

Pump Assembly   Motor (Vertical-Shaft)

DIRECT-REVERSING VERTICAL MACHINES

Dishwasher Tub

Pump Assembly   Drive Belt   Motor (Vertical-Shaft)

MAYTAG ONLY

Dishwasher Tub

Pump Suction

Pump Assembly   Motor (Horizontal-Shaft)

HORIZONTAL-SHAFT SINGLE-DIRECTION MACHINES

1-3 BRANDS

Figuring out what company made your dishwasher can be mildly confusing. Several big name companies bought their machines from different manufacturers at different times. One company, D&M, made machines for a LOT of different companies; you might find a D&M machine with any one of a couple of dozen different brand names on it. If the brand name of your machine is not listed directly in this manual, check the following listings for your brand:

D&M: This company made machines under a lot of different labels, including Admiral, Caloric, Chambers, Frigidaire, Gaffers & Sattler, Gibson, Kelvinator, Kenmore, Magic Chef, Modern Maid, Norge, Philco, Roper, Westinghouse, and a host of others.

FRIGIDAIRE: WCI

HOTPOINT: GE

IN-SINK-ERATOR (ISE): Kitchenaid

JENN-AIRE: Maytag

KITCHENAID: For many years they had their own distinctive design. A few years ago, Whirlpool bought Kitchenaid, and now these machines resemble Whirlpool machines in pump removal and service.

KELVINATOR: WCI or D&M.

KENMORE: Some were D&M, some are Whirlpool vertical machines.

MAGIC CHEF: Some are GE machines, some are Maytag, some are D&M.

O'KEEFE & MERRITT: WCI or D&M.

TAPPAN: WCI or D&M

ROPER: Whirlpool or D&M.

WASTE KING: Thermador

WESTINGHOUSE: WCI

Chapter 2

TROUBLESHOOTING TOOLS AND SAFETY TIPS AND TRICKS

2-1 BEFORE YOU START

Find yourself a good appliance parts dealer. You can find them in the yellow pages under the following headings:

- Appliances, Household, Major
- Appliances, Parts and Supplies
- Refrigerators, Domestic
- Appliances, Household, Repair and Service

Call a few of them and ask if they are a repair service, or if they sell parts, or both. Ask them if they offer free advice with the parts they sell. (Occasionally, stores that offer both parts and service will not want to give you advice.) Often the parts counter men are ex-technicians who got tired of the pressures of in-home service. They can be your best friends. However, you don't want to badger them with too many questions, so know your basics before you start asking questions.

Some parts houses may offer service, too. Be careful! There may be a conflict of interest. They may try to talk you out of even trying to fix your own dishwasher. They'll tell you it's too complicated, then in the same breath "guide" you to their service department. Who are you gonna believe, me or them? Not all service and parts places are this way, however. If they genuinely try to help you fix it yourself, and you find that you're unable to, they may be the best place to look for service. Here's a hot tip: after what I just said, if they sold you this book, then I'll just about guarantee they're genuinely interested in helping do-it-yourselfers.

When you go into the store, have ready the make, model and serial number from the nameplate of the dishwasher.

NAMEPLATE INFORMATION

The metal nameplate is usually found inside the door as shown in figure 2-A. It may also be fastened to the top edge of the door itself.

If you cannot find the nameplate, check the original papers that came with your dishwasher when it was new. They should contain the model number somewhere.

In any case, and especially if you have absolutely NO information about your dishwasher anywhere, make sure you bring your old part to the parts store with you. Sometimes they can match it up by looks or by part number.

2-2 PREVENTIVE MAINTENANCE

It's important to know that washing dishes in a dishwasher is not just a matter of blowing hot water at them. It is not just simply a mechanical or hydraulic process. It is also a *chemical* process. The chemicals you use, from detergent to rinse agent, are extremely critical. I recommend you use the following stuff regularly:

1) Use dry (powder) Cascade. The real stuff. Do not use liquid detergent. And *especially* do not use regular liquid dishsoap.

2) Use Jet-Dry® and check it regularly. Jet-Dry® causes water to sheet and run off the dishes, instead of beading up and spotting them. Also use a product called Glass Magic® to assist in preventing filming of the glass surfaces or calcium buildup.

3) If you live in an area with hard water, be on the lookout for any white film buildup you may get in the tub. It may be most obvious on any black plastic parts inside. This is primarily calcium. It can make plastic parts brittle and cause abrasion in moving parts, as well as spotting or filming on the dishes themselves. If you observe such buildup, periodically put about 1/4 to 1/2 cup of Lime-Away® or Citric Acid (usually available at drugstores) in the machine and run it through a wash cycle, with or without dishes. Repeat as often as necessary.

In extreme cases of hard-water buildup, run 1/2 cup of white vinegar through a single rinse-and-drain cycle, without any dishes in the machine.

These are pretty specific product endorsements for me to make without getting paid to make them, don't you think? To be totally honest, there are other chemicals which may be "good enough." But why bother? The "good stuff" only costs a few pennies more, and furthermore, it can be found in just about any grocery store in the nation.

See chapter 3 for a more in-depth discussion of wash quality and its factors.

A few more pearls of wisdom:

Every few months, do a thorough cleaning. Pay special attention to any buildup of detergent around door seals, especially along the bottom edge of the door. Also be on the lookout for cloudy film or calcium buildup.

Every six months or so, open the kickplate and check for leaks. Also exercise the hot water shutoff valve under the sink, to make sure it will close when you need it to.

Every few months, open, check and if necessary, clean out the air gap. (See Chapter 3 for diagram)

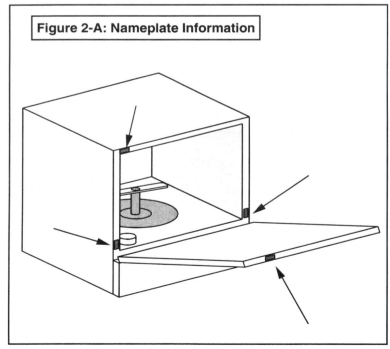

Figure 2-A: Nameplate Information

Be sure you load the dishwasher properly. Cups, glasses, bowls, etc. should be upside-down so they don't hold water. Large items must be loaded so they do not block the waterjets from the spray arms, or block the spray arms themselves as they rotate. Silverware should be secure.

Re-coat or replace any rusty dishracks. You can purchase a paint-on dishwasher rack coating from your appliance parts dealer or local hardware store. Replacing rusty dishracks costs a bit, but a pump leak caused by rusty grit getting into the pump seals can cost you more.

2-3 TROUBLESHOOTING

POOR WASH QUALITY

This is the most common complaint in a dishwasher. It covers a lot of different specific symptoms, from spotting, film or etching of the dishes to food left on dishes. It is discussed in detail in Chapter 3.

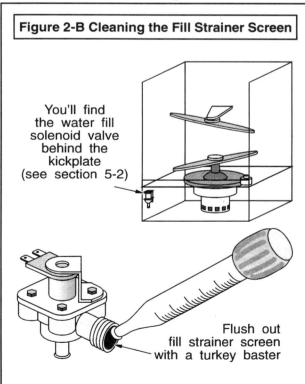

Figure 2-B Cleaning the Fill Strainer Screen

You'll find the water fill solenoid valve behind the kickplate (see section 5-2)

Flush out fill strainer screen with a turkey baster

NO POWER; MOTOR WON'T START

First check the house breaker or fuse.

Next, make sure that the dishwasher is plugged into the correct wall socket. (See the note in section 5-2 for an explanation)

The door is interlocked so that no fill or wash can occur while it's open. Check that the door locking lever is fully closed; this will close the door switch. Also check that the door switch is not defective as described in section 6-2(a).

Is the motor buzzing as described in section 6-2(c)? If so, the motor is locked up. It may be that something is jamming the pump. It may also be that the pump or motor bearings are bad, or the motor windings are fried; see Chapter 5.

Also check the junction box for burnt terminals; see section 6-2(e).

NO FILL

This is usually a defective water valve solenoid or clogged water valve. Try cleaning out the strainer screen as shown in figure 2-B; also test the solenoid for continuity. (Note that some Kitchenaid machines have a dual solenoid valve, with two solenoids. These valves should be tested as if they were two separate valves in series.) Replace the valve if defective.

When replacing the fill valve, use an O.E.M. part, or at least make sure the flow control washer is the same as in the original machine. Aftermarket parts may have a different flow control washer, which can cause high or low waterfill in your machine.

It could also be caused by the anti-flood float switch being stuck or defective. Rarely, but possibly, it can be traced to a burned contact inside the timer. Test as described in section 6-2 (a) and (b).

NO DRAIN, MOTOR RUNNING

This usually shows up as poor wash quality (severe spotting) due to cold water. Usually something is clogging the drain line or the Air Gap (see section 3-1.)

In GE or Kitchenaid machines, the drain valve solenoid may not be operating. Check the solenoid and also the timer (which controls it) as described in sections 6-2(a) and (b).

Another possibility is that junk has gotten into the drain pump impeller, and the vanes are broken clean off. Disassemble the pump as described in Chapter 5 and check the impeller.

TUB FILLS, BUT NO WASH OR NO DRAIN (MOTOR NOT RUNNING)

If you hear the motor trying to start (buzzing and clicking as described in Chapter 6) something is locking it up. It may be jammed with bits of food or glass. It may also be that a starting winding is burnt out.

If the machine is direct-reversing and it does start in one direction but not the other, then a starting winding is definitely burnt.

Disassemble or remove the pump and motor unit as described in Chapter 5. Clear whatever is jamming it. If you suspect that the motor is bad, check it as described in section 6-2(b).

If you don't even hear the motor *trying* to start, the timer contacts may be burnt out. Test and repair as described in section 6-2(b).

There is a also a motor starting relay. If this fails, it will cause similar symptoms. Test as described in section 6-2(c) and replace if defective.

NOISY OPERATION

Usually it is caused by bits of broken glass or rust getting into the pump impeller or spray arms. It is also frequently caused by worn out bearings in the pump or electric motor. Wasted pump bearings are a notably common problem in Maytag machines.

Try removing the spray arms and clearing them of debris. This can be difficult, and it may be easier to replace them.

Take the pump housing apart as described in Chapter 5 and try turning the pump and motor shafts by hand. It should be smooth, without too much resistance. Any gritty feeling indicates bad bearings or stuff contacting the pump impeller.

TIMER NOT ADVANCING

Usually the timer motor has gone bad. But be sure to check the wiring diagram first, as described in Chapter 6. There may be several other switches in the circuit, for example thermostat or pushbutton selector switches.

The solution is to replace the defective motor or switch. If it's the timer, you may be able to get a rebuilt one to save a few bucks.

WATER LEAKING ONTO FLOOR

If water is coming out the front of the machine, it's usually leaky door seals, but there are a few other suspects. The wrong soap can cause suds, which can leak out even if the seals are good. There are also some designs, notably a certain Whirlpool "bladder" design, which can develop a water jet that blows water past the door seal. Check for these problems first. If you still suspect the door seal, try cleaning any accumulated detergent or other gunk from it. If you need to replace the seals, your parts dealer has a door seal kit. See Chapter 4 for a more in-depth discussion of these and other possible leak sources.

If water is coming from beneath the machine, it is usually coming from pump seals, but it could also be coming from a hose or from the fill or drain solenoid valve. Remove the kickplate and operate the machine while looking beneath it. Try to isolate the leak by watching where the water drips on the floor. Remember that there are live wires under there; don't stick your hands in there while the machine is plugged in. Diagnose and repair as described in chapters 4 or 5.

DOOR DETERGENT DISPENSERS NOT WORKING

If the detergent dispensers are not popping open, usually a solenoid or bi-metallic trigger has failed. Remove the outer door panel as described in section 5-2 and test as described in section 6-2(f). It may also be that they are gunked up with detergent or rinse agent. Clean them out thoroughly.

2-4 TOOLS (Figure 2-C)

The tools that you may need (depending on the diagnosis) are listed below. Some are optional. The reason for the option is explained.

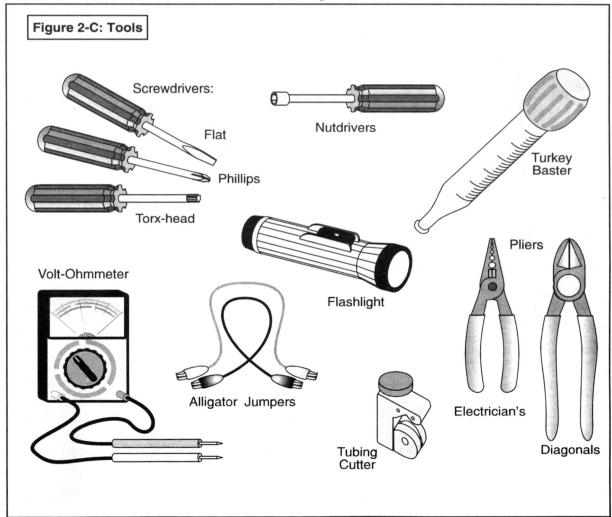

Figure 2-C: Tools

Screwdrivers:
Flat
Phillips
Torx-head
Nutdrivers
Turkey Baster
Volt-Ohmmeter
Flashlight
Alligator Jumpers
Pliers
Electrician's
Diagonals
Tubing Cutter

SCREWDRIVERS: Both flat and Phillips head; two or three sizes of each. It's best to have at least a stubby, 4- and 6-inch sizes. For certain late model machines, you will need a size 20 Torx-head screwdriver.

NUTDRIVERS: You will need at least 1/4" and 5/16" sizes. 4- or 6-inch ones should suffice, but it's better to have a stubby, too.

VOM (VOLT-OHM METER): For testing electrical circuits. If you do not have one, get one. An inexpensive one will suffice, as long as it has both "AC Voltage" and "Resistance" (i.e. Rx1, Rx10) settings on the dial. It will do for our purposes.

ELECTRICAL PLIERS or STRIPPERS and DIAGONAL CUTTING PLIERS: For cutting and stripping small electrical wire

COPPER TUBING CUTTER: If you need to remove the dishwasher from its space under the countertop, you may need to cut the copper water feed line slightly shorter to get a new fitting on when you reinstall the machine.

TURKEY BASTER: For flushing out water valves or draining water from pumps.

ALLIGATOR JUMPERS (sometimes called a "CHEATER" or "CHEATER WIRE":) Small gauge (14-16 gauge or so) and about 12-18 inches long, for testing electrical circuits. Available at your local electronics store. Cost: a few bucks for 4 or 5 of them.

BUTT CONNECTORS, CRIMPERS, WIRE NUTS and ELECTRICAL TAPE: For splicing small wire.

OPTIONAL TOOLS (Figure 2-D)

SNAP-AROUND AMMETER: For determining if electrical components are energized. Quite useful; but a bit expensive, and there are alternate methods. If you have one, use it; otherwise, don't bother getting one.

EXTENDIBLE INSPECTION MIRROR: For seeing difficult places beneath the dishwasher and behind panels.

CORDLESS POWER SCREWDRIVER OR DRILL/DRIVER WITH MAGNETIC SCREWDRIVER AND NUTDRIVER TIPS: For pulling off panels held in place by many screws. It can save you lots of time and hassle.

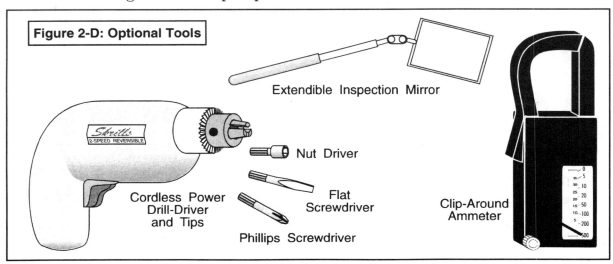

Figure 2-D: Optional Tools

Extendible Inspection Mirror

Nut Driver

Flat Screwdriver

Cordless Power Drill-Driver and Tips

Phillips Screwdriver

Clip-Around Ammeter

2-5 HOW TO USE A VOM AND AMMETER

Many home handymen are very intimidated by electricity. It's true that diagnosing and repairing electrical circuits requires a bit more care than most operations, due to the danger of getting shocked. But there is no mystery or voodoo about the things we'll be doing. Remember the rule in section 2-6 (1); while you are working on a circuit, energize the circuit only long enough to perform whatever test you're performing, then take the power back off it to perform the repair. You need not be concerned with any theory, like what an ohm is, or what a volt is. You will only need to be able to set the VOM onto the right scale, touch the test leads to the right place and read the meter.

In using the VOM (Volt-Ohm Meter) for our purposes, the two test leads are always plugged into the "+" and "-" holes on the VOM. (Some VOMs have more than two holes.)

2-5(a) TESTING VOLTAGE (Figure 2-E)

Set the dial of the VOM on the lowest VAC scale (A.C. Voltage) over 120 volts. For example, if there's a 50 setting and a 250 setting on the VAC dial, use the 250 scale, because 250 is the lowest setting over 120 volts.

Touch the two test leads to the two metal contacts of a live power source, like a wall outlet or the terminals of the motor that you're testing for voltage. (Do not jam the test leads into a wall outlet!) If you are getting power through the VOM, the meter will jump up and steady on a reading. You may have to convert the scale in your head. For example, if you're using the 250 volt dial setting and the meter has a "25" scale, simply divide by 10; 120 volts would be "12" on the meter.

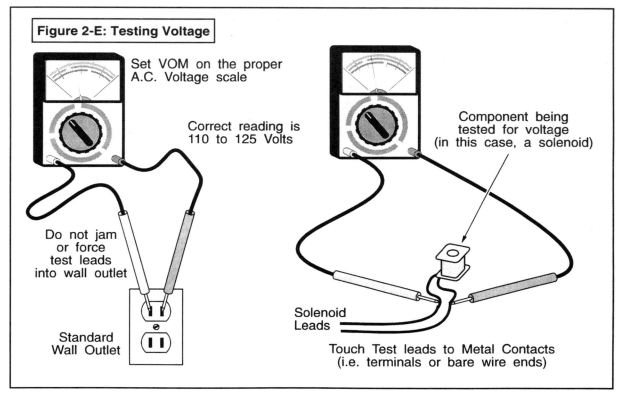

Figure 2-E: Testing Voltage

Set VOM on the proper A.C. Voltage scale

Correct reading is 110 to 125 Volts

Do not jam or force test leads into wall outlet

Standard Wall Outlet

Component being tested for voltage (in this case, a solenoid)

Solenoid Leads

Touch Test leads to Metal Contacts (i.e. terminals or bare wire ends)

2-5(b) TESTING FOR CONTINUITY (Figure 2-F)

Don't let the word "continuity" scare you. It's derived from the word "continuous." In an electrical circuit, electricity has to flow from a power source back to that power source. If there is any break in the circuit, it is not continuous, and it has no continuity. "Good" continuity means that there is no break in the circuit.

For example, if you were testing a solenoid to see if it was burned out, you would try putting a small amount of power through the solenoid. If it was burned out, there would be a break in the circuit, the electricity wouldn't flow, and your meter would show no continuity.

That is what the resistance part of your VOM does; it provides a small electrical current (using batteries within the VOM) and measures how fast the current is flowing. For our purposes, it doesn't matter how *fast* the current is flowing; only that there *is* current flow.

To use your VOM to test continuity, set the dial on (resistance) R x 1, or whatever the lowest setting is. Touch the metal parts of the test leads together and read the meter. It should peg the meter all the way on the right side of the scale, towards "0" on the meter's "resistance" or "ohms" scale. If the meter does not read zero ohms, adjust the thumbwheel on the front of the VOM until it does read zero. If you cannot get the meter to read zero, the battery in the VOM is low; replace it.

If you are testing, say, a solenoid, first make sure that the solenoid leads are not connected to anything, especially a power source. If the solenoid's leads are still connected to something, you may get a reading through that something. If there is still live power on the item you're testing for continuity, you will burn out your VOM instantly and possibly shock yourself.

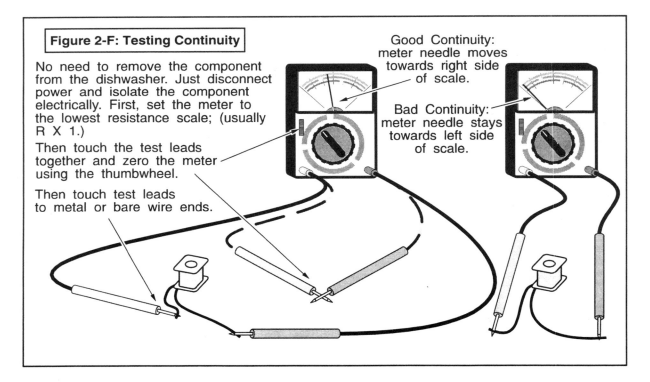

Figure 2-F: Testing Continuity

No need to remove the component from the dishwasher. Just disconnect power and isolate the component electrically. First, set the meter to the lowest resistance scale; (usually R X 1.)

Then touch the test leads together and zero the meter using the thumbwheel.

Then touch test leads to metal or bare wire ends.

Good Continuity: meter needle moves towards right side of scale.

Bad Continuity: meter needle stays towards left side of scale.

Touch the two test leads to the two bare wire ends or terminals of the solenoid. You can touch the ends of the wires and test leads with your hands if necessary to get better contact. The voltage that the VOM batteries put out is very low, and you will not be shocked. If there is NO continuity, the meter won't move. If there is GOOD continuity, the meter will move toward the right side of the scale and steady on a reading. This is the resistance reading and it doesn't concern us; we only care that we show good continuity. If the meter moves only very little and stays towards the left side of the scale, that's BAD continuity; the solenoid is no good.

If you are testing a switch, you will show little or no resistance (good continuity) when the switch is closed, and NO continuity when the switch is open. If you do not, the switch is bad.

2-5(c) AMMETERS

Ammeters are a little bit more complex to explain without going into a lot of electrical theory. If you own an ammeter, you probably already know how to use it.

If you don't, don't get one. Ammeters are expensive. And for our purposes, there are other ways to determine what an ammeter tests for. If you don't own one, skip this section.

For our purposes, ammeters are simply a way of testing for continuity without having to cut into the system or to disconnect power from whatever it is we're testing.

Ammeters measure the current in amps flowing through a wire. The greater the current that's flowing through a wire, the greater the density of the magnetic field, or flux, it produces around the wire. The ammeter simply measures the density of this flux, and thus the amount of current, flowing through the wire. To determine continuity, for our purposes, we can simply isolate the component that we're testing (so we do not accidentally measure the current going through any other components) and see if there's *any* current flow.

To use your ammeter, first make sure that it's on an appropriate scale (0 to 10 or 20 amps will do). Isolate a wire leading directly to the component you're testing. Put the ammeter loop around that wire and read the meter. (Figure 2-G)

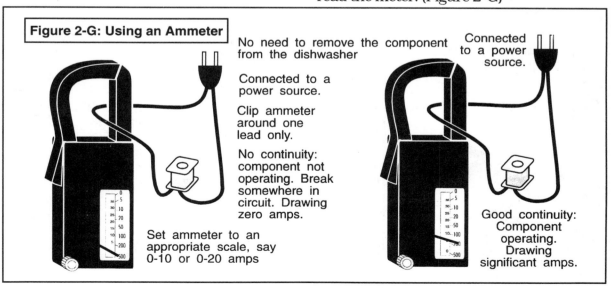

Figure 2-G: Using an Ammeter

No need to remove the component from the dishwasher

Connected to a power source.

Clip ammeter around one lead only.

No continuity: component not operating. Break somewhere in circuit. Drawing zero amps.

Set ammeter to an appropriate scale, say 0-10 or 0-20 amps

Connected to a power source.

Good continuity: Component operating. Drawing significant amps.

For example, let's say you're trying to tell if a motor is trying to start, but you think the motor is locked up. A locked motor that's trying to start uses one heckuva lot of electricity (see Section 6-2(c)) and cycles in and out every minute or two on the overload switch. To confirm your diagnosis, clamp the ammeter around one motor lead or even just one of your main wall power leads. If the meter shows you drawing 10 to 20 amps for a few seconds, then nothing for a minute or two (when the overload cuts the circuit,) you've got a locked motor.

2-6 BASIC REPAIR AND SAFETY PRECAUTIONS

1) Always de-energize (pull the plug or trip the breaker on) any dishwasher that you're disassembling. If you need to re-energize the dishwasher to perform a test, make sure any bare wires or terminals are taped or insulated. Energize the unit only long enough to perform whatever test you're performing, then disconnect the power again.

2) If the manual advocates replacing the part, REPLACE IT!! You might find, say, a solenoid that has jammed for no apparent reason. Sometimes you can clean it out and lubricate it, and get it going again. The key words here are *"apparent reason."*

There is a reason that it stopped—you can bet on it—and if you get it going and re-install it, you are running a very high risk that it will stop again. If that happens, you will have to start repairing your dishwasher all over again. It may only act up when it is hot, or it may be bent slightly...there are a hundred different "what if's." Very few of the parts mentioned in this book will cost you over ten or twenty dollars. Replace the part.

3) Always replace the green (ground) leads when you remove an electrical component. They're there for a reason. And NEVER EVER remove the third (ground) prong in the main power plug!

4) When opening the dishwasher cabinet or console, remember that the sheet metal parts have very sharp edges. Wear gloves, and be careful not to cut your hands!

5) When testing for your power supply from a wall outlet, plug in a small appliance such as a shaver or blow dryer. If you're not getting full power out of the outlet, you'll know it right away.

6) If you have diagnosed a certain part to be bad, but you cannot figure out how to remove it, sometimes it helps to get the new part and examine it for mounting holes or other clues as to how it may be mounted.

Chapter 3

WASH QUALITY PROBLEMS

NOTE: This chapter assumes that the motor is running and you hear water whooshing around inside the machine. If not, go back to chapter 2 and troubleshoot!!!

Poor wash quality mainly involves heavy spotting and filming or etching of the dishes. It can usually be traced to cold water or excessively hot, hard or soft water, poor detergent, or inadequate drying.

Washing dishes in a dishwasher is not just a matter of blowing hot water at them. It is *not* just simply a mechanical or hydraulic process. It is also a *chemical* process. The chemicals you use, from detergent to rinse agent, are extremely critical. And the temperature of the water that dissolves and carries these chemicals is critical as well.

Note, however, that there are a few things that are prone to spotting even if your dishwasher is operating perfectly. Teflon®, for example, has a relatively porous surface that holds water, then sort of oozes it back out later. It is difficult to air dry and it usually must be wiped with a towel. Certain kinds of plastic have similar properties. See section 3-2.

3-1 TROUBLESHOOTING

SPOTTING

It is CRITICAL to have wash and rinse water at around 150 degrees, plus or minus ten degrees. Any cooler, and the detergent will not dissolve properly, resulting in spotting or filming. If the dishwasher has a heater, the fill water may be just a little cooler, as low as 125, but it should be at least 140 well before the end of each cycle. The heater is not designed to heat *cold* water; it is designed to *maintain* water temperature.

To test the temperature, Turn a glass upright so it will collect water and put a candy thermometer into it. Let it run in the wash cycle for at least five minutes, then open the door and see what the temperature is.

If the dishwasher is installed right next to the kitchen sink, as it is in most installations, you can run water out the sink and test the temperature there. If you do, however, take note of how long the sink faucet runs cold before hot water starts running out. And try to note how many gallons of cold water this amounts to. That's roughly how many gallons of cold water that are entering your dishwasher before any hot water gets there.

If your water temperature is too cool, you have several options, depending on the cause. You can try turning up the water heater temperature; sometimes this is enough. But to my experience, water fill temperature problems are usually caused by the dishwasher being installed too far away from the water heater. The tub fills with only a gallon or two of water; by the time the hot water gets from the heater to the dishwasher, the tub is at least half full of cold water. If the dishwasher water feed line comes off the same line that feeds the

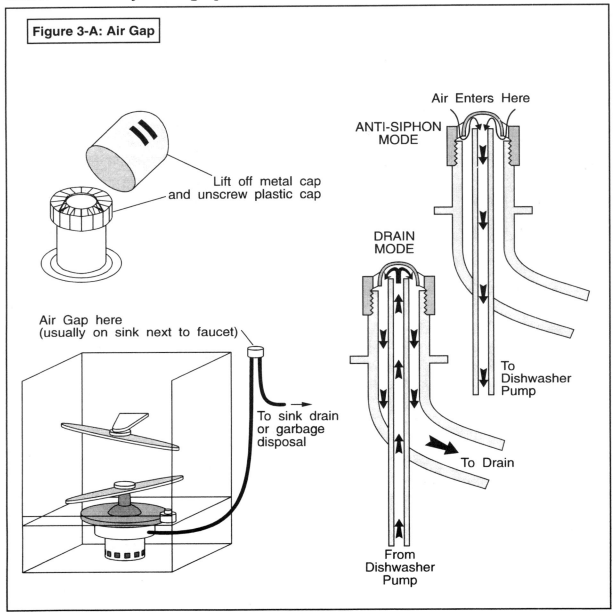

Figure 3-A: Air Gap

Lift off metal cap and unscrew plastic cap

Air Gap here (usually on sink next to faucet)

To sink drain or garbage disposal

Air Enters Here

ANTI-SIPHON MODE

DRAIN MODE

To Dishwasher Pump

To Drain

From Dishwasher Pump

sink, it may help to warm up the line by running water out the hot water sink faucet before starting the dishwasher. However, the hot water line may cool off again between the wash and rinse cycles, so you may need to leave the sink valve cracked open a little to keep the line warm. This wastes a tremendous amount of water.

It's a tough problem, and solving it can involve re-designing the entire water system in your house. Before you do that, you might consider installing a small instant water heater nearer to the dishwasher. There are several small heaters available that heat just a few gallons and are made to be installed beneath the sink. Ask your appliance parts dealer or check your local hardware store.

About the worst case of water temperature problems I ever saw was caused by an improper installation. The complaint was water spots on the dishes. Whomever installed the dishwasher had left too much rubber drain hose connected, and when the dishwasher was pushed back into place beneath the counter, the drain hose kinked badly. The old, cold water would never drain out of the tub at the beginning of the cycle, and thus it would not fill with new hot water. (The anti-flood float switch would prevent overfill.) Incidentally, it had been installed two years before, and the people had been trying to use it regularly since then. Thus, in addition to that two-year-old cold water in the bottom of the tub, there was also two years' worth of detergent and disgusting, moldy leftovers. The solution was to simply cut the drain hose shorter, but I have no idea how many cycles it took to melt all that gunk out of the tub. I also have no idea why it took them two years to call me.

AIR GAP

There is also an anti-siphon device, called an air gap, built into the drain line. It is required by law in most installations. It prevents accidental backflow (siphoning) into the dishwasher from the house drain lines. A typical air gap re-directs water 180 degrees, and thus it has constrictions that can easily trap a chunk of food trying to pass through it.

Symptoms are the same as for any other blockage of the drain line, except that you may also see water flowing out of the air gap vents directly into the sink.

Fortunately, they are pretty easy to open and clean. (See figure 3-A) In most installations, it is a little chrome or brass blob with a couple of vent holes in it, sitting right next to your sink faucet handles. If it's not there, find the hose that drains your dishwasher into the sink trap or garbage disposal, and trace it back directly to the air gap.

Usually all that's involved in cleaning it is to pull off the little chrome blob and unscrew the top of the air gap itself. Both drain pipes will be exposed.

CLOGGING OF THE WATER SYSTEM

The pump suction screen or spray arms can become clogged by hard water lime or by bits of food or glass from broken dishes.

To diagnose, remove the spray arm assembly as shown in Chapter 3 and shake it. Any bits of glass or other debris will make a noisy clatter. Try to remove them. It can be difficult; it's a lot like trying to fish coins out of a piggy bank. If it's too hard, just replace the spray arm.

If you have a lime or hard water buildup clogging any water holes, run some Lime-Away® through your machine as described in section 2-2, preventive maintenance.

POOR DETERGENT OR RINSE AGENT

Yup, you get what you pay for. Use acidic or hard detergent, and you *will* have problems and you *will* shorten the life of your machine significantly. I know you don't want to hear me say that, but when it comes to dishwashers it's really true; even more so than with other machines. It doesn't pay to cut corners on what you put into your dishwasher. C'mon, now, I always tell you when you can "economize," right? Trust me here. Don't be cheap. You can save a few pennies now, but it will cost you dollars later.

Here's the scoop: Use dry (powder) Cascade®. The real stuff. Do not use liquid detergent. In my opinion, they have not yet figured out how to make liquid detergent that dissolves properly. And *especially* do not use regular liquid dishsoap. It is made to suds up, which you do not want in a dishwasher.

Also use Jet-Dry® and check it regularly. Jet-Dry® causes water to sheet and run off the dishes, instead of beading up and spotting them.

Also use a product called Glass Magic® regularly to assist in preventing filming or etching of the glass surfaces. Put a mixture of about 1/3 Glass Magic® to about 2/3 powdered Cascade® in the pop-open door dispenser. This will open and dispense the mixture during the *second* wash cycle.

Calcium buildup and acidity do not just affect how your dishes look. Look, if acid is eating and calcium is abrading the glass in your dishes, what do you think those chemicals are doing to the working parts of your machine, under high-temperature and high-pressure conditions?

ACID ETCHING

Etching of your glassware is damage of a more permanent nature. In early stages, the glassware may have an iridescent blue, pink or purplish look when you hold it under the light in a certain way. In later stages, the glass takes on a cloudy or milky appearance, or it may even be pitted. These cannot be removed by any amount of scrubbing. This later stage should not be confused with filming, which can be removed by a little Lime-Away®, Glass Magic® or white vinegar.

Etching is caused by overly acidic conditions inside your dishwasher. It does not seem to be related to the cost or quality of the glass. Softened water tends to be acidic to begin with. Softened water at excessively high temperature and in combination with lots of detergent seems to be the conditions most conducive to acid etching.

If you have soft water, make sure it is entering the dishwasher at a temperature below 150 degrees. Also try cutting the amount of detergent you use in half. (Make sure the dishes are still being cleaned and sterilized, of course!) Realize, however, that some types of glass seem to be prone to etching no matter what you do.

DRYER BLOWER INOPERATIVE

Excessive spotting may mean the dryer blower or heater is not working. Test the motor or heater as described in section 6-2(d) and (g) and replace if defective.

IMPROPER LOADING

Loading the dishwasher improperly can cause all sorts of problems, from blockage of the waterspray to dish or pump damage. Make sure the dishes are loaded properly as described in section 2-2, preventive maintenance.

3-2 NO PROBLEM, MON!

There are certain types of dishes that you should NOT wash in your dishwasher under any circumstances. For example, certain kinds of "darkening" in fine silverware is normal, and does not indicate a problem with your dishwasher. Other things to watch out for:

Cutlery with wood, bone or horn handles may crack or break or split under high temperatures and/or hydraulic pressure.

The high-pressure hot water jets may also be enough to wash the hand painting off your hand-painted china.

Lacquerware, genuine antique milkglass, or anodized aluminum may discolor.

Iron skillets or pans may rust. Any rust that comes off is also very abrasive and will not be good for the pump and seals.

Antique or very delicate crystal or china can break easily under high temperatures and pressures.

Chapter 4

WATER LEAKS

There are two general areas where you will commonly find water leaking from a dishwasher.

The first is from around the door; water will generally show up on the kitchen floor in front of the dishwasher.

The second is from some component under the tub. The most common sources are pump seals and water valves, though it really can come from just about anything else under there, such as heater mounts, float switches, dryer fans, hoses, etc.

A slow, under-tub leak may go years without being detected. Often the tile or linoleum in front of the dishwasher is slightly raised, and water does not flow up-hill. A slow leak beneath the tub can rot a wooden floor or cabinetry. It can also cause odors, mildew, etc. Often the first sign you might see is water leaking under the cabinetry and into the space beneath the kitchen sink.

It pays to pull off the kickplate every six months or so and look around under there with a flashlight for any sign of a drip. Do it while the machine is running. Also check the hot water shutoff valve beneath the sink for leaks, and exercise it; open and close it a couple of times and make sure it works so that you will be able to shut it off when you need to.

A third source of water "leakage" (though it really isn't a leak) is from the air gap. The air gap is an anti-backflow device installed in the drain line, to prevent the dishwasher from accidentally siphoning fluid from your house's sewer line back into the dishwasher tub. If this air gap or the house's drain line becomes clogged, water can run out of the air vent, and generally it runs straight into your sink. Note, however, that this will only occur when the dishwasher is operating in the "pump out" mode, trying to drain the tub. There is an illustration and discussion of the air gap in section 3-1.

4-1 SUDS

Using the wrong detergent can cause sudsing during the wash cycle. When this happens, the suds may rise above the level of, or be splashed over the door sill. It usually shows up as a drip, and not as suds on the floor.

To diagnose, open the door during a wash cycle and look inside. A high level of suds will be obvious to you.

The solution is to change detergents. I highly recommend powdered Cascade® detergent. See section 2-2, preventive maintenance.

To get through the cycle you've already started without spilling too much more water, try adding a couple of tablespoons of cooking oil to the wash cycle. The oil will knock down the suds and it will be washed out during the rinse cycle.

4-2 DOOR SEALS

If you do not see any physical damage or excessive soap scum buildup on the door seals, it is rare for them to be the source of a leak.

If you think they are leaking, try cleaning them first. Really get in there and get all the built-up detergent and gunk out of there. Pay particular attention to the area around the inside bottom of the door; it tends to collect detergent build-up, food particles and soap scum. Use Lime-Away® or full-strength white vinegar as described in section 3-1 to remove any hard-water calcium buildup.

A particular Whirlpool machine was designed with a "bladder," or expandable rubber chamber, at the top of the water tower. This bladder expands under water pressure to mate the tower with the upper

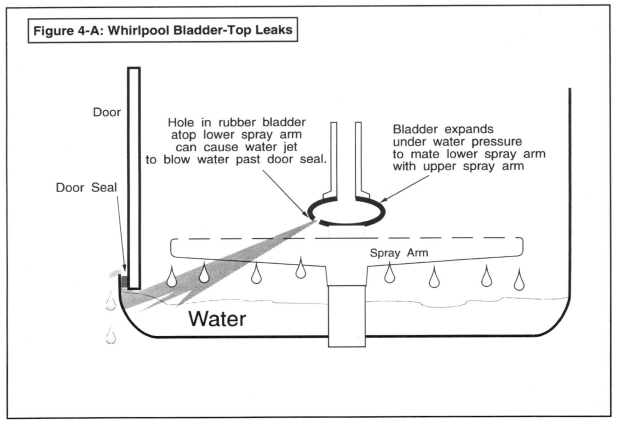

Figure 4-A: Whirlpool Bladder-Top Leaks

Door

Door Seal

Hole in rubber bladder atop lower spray arm can cause water jet to blow water past door seal.

Bladder expands under water pressure to mate lower spray arm with upper spray arm

Spray Arm

Water

spray arm. (See figure 4-A) These bladders can develop holes. A jet of water may shoot out of the holes, and no matter how good the door seal is, the waterjet will blow right past it, causing an apparent "leak." To replace the bladder, simply unscrew it from the top of the spray arms.

4-3 WATER VALVE

Remove the kick plate as described in section 5-2 and look at the water inlet solenoid valve.

On occasion, the guts of the water valve may rot out.

This usually shows up as a very slow drip coming from the top of the water valve solenoid. (See figure 4-B.) If the leak has been going on for a while, there may also be traces of rust or mineral deposits on top of the solenoid.

The solution is to shut off the water supply and replace the valve.

On rare occasions, the diaphragm within a water valve has been known to rupture. When this occurs, water will start filling the tub and will not stop. The anti-flood float switch will not close the valve. All it does is shut off the valve electrically, and this is not an electrical problem. The water will continue flowing no matter how much runs out onto the kitchen floor. Better hope it doesn't happen while you're not home!

The solution is to shut off the water supply and replace the valve.

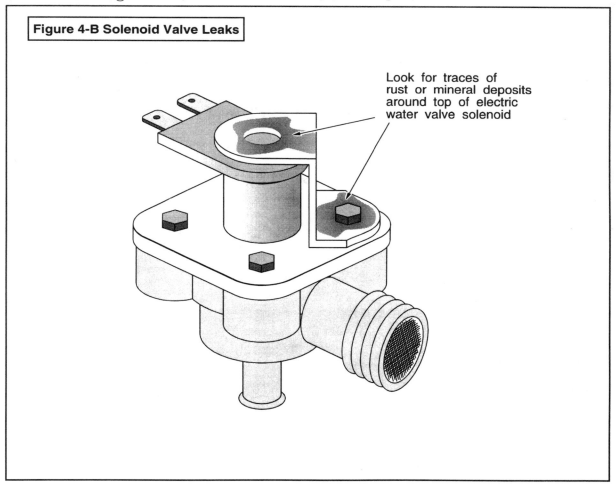

Figure 4-B Solenoid Valve Leaks

Look for traces of rust or mineral deposits around top of electric water valve solenoid

4-4 PUMP SEALS

Pump seals get worn out. Just a fact of life. Rubber seal...metal shaft...you get the picture. Throw in some tiny bits of broken glass, plastic, nutshells, seeds, and other assorted abrasives over the years, and it's a wonder they last as long as they do. Bits of rust from your rusty dishracks can really accelerate the process.

Pump seal leaks will show up as water dripping from the motor. (From the pump pulley in Maytag machines.) It may also get slung around a bit from a rotating pump shaft.

The solution is to rebuild the pump. In some designs, you pull the whole motor and pump unit and replace it with a new or rebuilt unit. See Chapter 5 for details.

4-5 HOSES, HEATERS, BLOWERS AND OTHER MISCELLANEOUS UNDER-TUB SOURCES

On rare occasions, the leak will be coming from the sealing washers around tub heater mounts, dryer blower gaskets, or other small tub penetrations. You need to replace the gasket or seal. Drain or recirculation hoses have been known to get old and brittle and crack open. Replace the hose.

In sidewinder machines with butterfly drain valves, such as GE and Westinghouse machines, (see section 1-2) you may get a leak from the drain valve stem. In most of these, this means pulling out the whole pump and motor unit and replacing it with a rebuilt unit as described in chapter 5.

Kitchenaid machines have a solenoid drain valve which can also develop leaks. See section 4-3.

Chapter 5

PUMP AND MOTOR PROBLEMS

Okay, you've diagnosed out every other possibility, and it just has to be the pump and/or motor that's gone haywire. How do we get into it? How do we disassemble it? Do we need to remove the unit from its space under the counter?

These are the questions this chapter answers.

5-1 GETTING THE PUMP OUT

In some machines it is easier pull the whole machine out from under the kitchen counter to get to the pump or the motor. Specifically: GE/Hotpoint, Thermador/Waste King, late model Whirlpool, and WCI/Westinghouse.

In yet other machines, the pump and motor can both be easily removed with the machine in place. Specifically: D&M, Maytag, ISE/Kitchenaid, and Whirlpool Vertical Machines.

D&M, Kitchenaid, and Thermador pumps can easily be rebuilt with the machine in place, but getting the motor out can be a bit persnickety. Give it a try, but if you have trouble getting the motor out or back in, remove the machine.

5-2 TYPICAL DISHWASHER INSTALLATION, MOUNTING, REMOVAL, and CABINET ACCESS

Most dishwasher problems can be diagnosed and fixed with the machine in place. However, some problems cannot. In either case, you'll usually need to get to the components beneath the tub. This section describes cabinet access and removal of a built-in machine.

Most built-in models are built with removable kickplates as shown in Figure 5-A. Removing this kickplate as shown allows access to the fill valve, electrical junction box, and drive motor. Most built-in models are also fastened to the countertop by two screws at the front of the machine; open the door to access these screws.

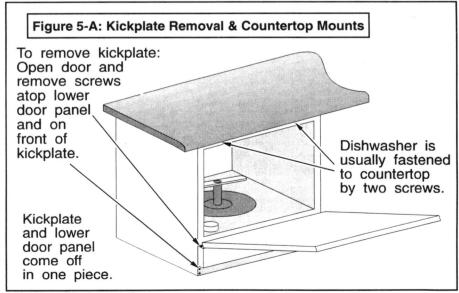

Figure 5-A: Kickplate Removal & Countertop Mounts

To remove kickplate: Open door and remove screws atop lower door panel and on front of kickplate.

Kickplate and lower door panel come off in one piece.

Dishwasher is usually fastened to countertop by two screws.

To get to the timer, selector switches, detergent dispenser trigger, wiring diagram or anything else located inside the door, remove the screws holding on the front panel as shown in figure 5-B.

Before you can remove the entire dishwasher from its mounting location, you must disconnect three things: the hot water fill line, the water drain line, and the electrical power supply.

Disconnect the electrical connection first. It is usually pretty easy. Though some are hard-wired into the wall, most dishwashers are plugged into a regular outlet beneath the kitchen sink. If you are unlucky enough to have one that's hard-wired, you must shut off the breaker and disconnect the main power cord at the junction box. This box is usually located just inside the kickplate on the front corner of the machine (see Figure 5-C).

NOTE: If your machine is plugged in beneath the sink, make sure you get the plug back into the correct outlet. Usually the other outlet beneath the sink is for the garbage disposal, which is wired through a switch near the sink. Normally the garbage disposal switch is off, so there is no power to its outlet; if you plug the dishwasher into that outlet, it will not run at all. I cannot begin to tell you how many times I've been called to fix a "dead" dishwasher, when the only problem was that it was plugged into the wrong outlet. (At 30-50 bucks per service call, that's an expensive mistake)

The drain line is also usually pretty easy to disconnect. It is normally connected to the sink drain by flexible rubber hose and hose clamps. But don't forget that there may still be water in the pump and drain line, even if the tub is empty! Have a shal-

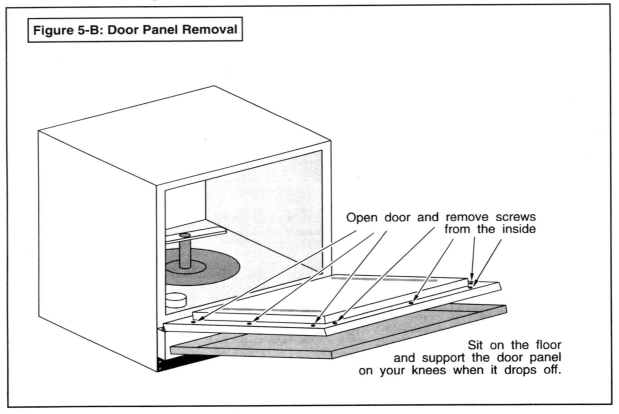

Figure 5-B: Door Panel Removal

Open door and remove screws from the inside

Sit on the floor and support the door panel on your knees when it drops off.

low pan or an old towel standing by (one that will fit beneath the pump drain connection) to catch any water left in the tub or drain line.

The fill line is another story. It is usually copper-piped right up to the fill valve. This makes it less likely to fail and flood the kitchen, but it can also make it more difficult to remove and install. If you disconnect the copper line from the valve, you may have to cut it shorter to get rid of the old brass connection fittings. Make sure you have enough copper line remaining to re-connect it to the valve. A better alternative (though it's not always possible) may be to leave the copper line connected to the valve, and disconnect the valve from the rest of the dishwasher. Of course, if you're replacing the valve, it doesn't really matter; you've got to disconnect the copper line, anyway.

Figure 5-C: Electrical Junction Box

Junction Box is usually located beneath the kickplate towards the front of the machine on either the left or right side.

THE FOLLOWING PAGES HAVE DISASSEMBLY PROCEDURES AND NOTES FOR THE EIGHT MOST COMMON MACHINE DESIGNS TODAY.

SPECIFIC MODELS MAY VARY SLIGHTLY, BUT YOUR MACHINE SHOULD LOOK VERY SIMILAR TO ONE OF THESE. PLEASE NOTE, HOWEVER, THAT THERE MAY BE PARTS PRESENT ON YOUR MACHINE THAT ARE NOT ON THESE ILLUSTRATIONS. THEREFORE, WHEN DISASSEMBLING YOUR MACHINE, CAREFULLY NOTE HOW ALL PARTS ARE INSTALLED AND IN WHAT ORDER THEY COME OFF.

WHIRLPOOL VERTICAL MACHINES

TECH NOTES

Vertical Whirlpool machines are direct reversing, two-impeller machines.

The whole pump and motor unit are easily removed with the machine in place.

The pump can be rebuilt. Your appliance parts dealer has impeller and seal kits. However, if the top motor bearing is damaged, the whole pump and motor unit must be replaced. When you get the pump disassembled, turn the motor by hand. If it's at all sticky or gritty, replace the motor.

If you have a bladder-top design, it has been replaced with a re-designed system. A new pump and motor unit will come with the new design.

TECH TIPS

Unplug the machine and remove the kickplate. Disconnect the motor wiring harness plug. Disconnect the drain hose from the pump unit and be prepared to catch any water left in the pump. Unscrew the drain check valve from the pump body. Twist the pump unit retaining blocks inward and lift out the whole pump and motor unit. It might be sticky; you can rock it a bit to loosen it. Do NOT pry the seal or remove the big seal from the pump body.

Installation is the opposite of removal. Make sure you line up the pump drain port with the notch in the tub. The seal may not want to go into the tub; smear it with a very thin coat of vegetable oil (VERY thin!) to help it slide into place. Make sure it is centered and seated evenly. When you get the pump/motor unit back into place and hooked up, pour a gallon of water into the tub before starting the machine. Do not run the pump dry!!!

Wash Pump Cover

Seal

Valve Cover

Valve Spring

Valve

Separator

Ball Check

Seal

Inlet Base

Bushing

Seal

Drain Pump Cover

Drain Impeller

Pump Seal

Pump Base

Tub Seal

Drain Check Valve

Drive Motor

Wash Impeller

Strainer

Macerator & Spring

Sleeve

Twist the rubber retaining blocks out of the way to lift the pump and motor unit out of the tub.

BLADDER-TOP MACHINES are slightly different inside, but they are disassembled similarly

Spray Arm

Bladder (Unscrew to remove)

Spray Arm Bearing

To remove tower: Pry up tab and twist the tower to unlock it from the pump base.

Pump Base

Tub Seal

Drain Check Valve

Drive Motor

WHIRLPOOL VERTICAL MACHINES

WHIRLPOOL HORIZONTAL MACHINES

TECH NOTES

Late-model Whirlpool (sidewinders) are direct-reversing horizontal-shaft machines. When the motor reverses, the drain valve automatically opens to drain the tub.

You usually need to remove these machines from under the kitchen counter to remove the pump and motor unit.

Your appliance parts dealer has a seal kit to rebuild the pump.

TECH TIPS

These are very straightforward machines to disassemble. Disconnect the motor harness, all hoses, the motor mount and the pump suction inlet. Have a shallow pan or an old towel standing by to catch any water when you remove the hoses.

The only trick is that the screws holding it together are Torx-head screws, so you need a size 20 Torx-head screwdriver.

To get the impeller and seal out, unscrew the pump disk from the pump inlet with a pair of pliers. Don't forget to remove the drain cover and check the rubber diaphragm.

When installing the motor into the pump housing, make sure the flat on the motor shaft matches the flat in the impeller.

When you get the pump/motor unit back into place and hooked up, pour a gallon of water into the tub before starting the machine. Do not run the pump dry!!!

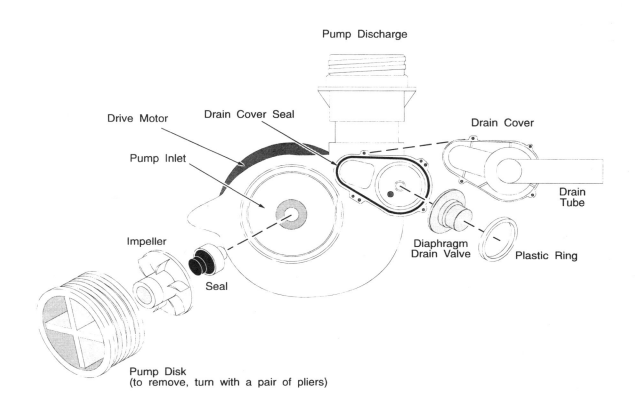

Pump Discharge

Drive Motor

Drain Cover Seal

Drain Cover

Pump Inlet

Drain Tube

Impeller

Diaphragm Drain Valve

Plastic Ring

Seal

Pump Disk
(to remove, turn with a pair of pliers)

WHIRLPOOL LATE-MODEL HORIZONTAL MACHINES

GE / HOTPOINT

TECH NOTES

General Electric and Hotpoint machines are single-direction, horizontal-shaft machines. To change from wash mode to drain mode, a solenoid-operated flapper valve closes off the spray arms and opens the drain port.

You usually need to remove the machine from beneath the countertop to remove the pump and motor unit.

If the motor is not starting, you may be able to free it by hand. Unplug the machine, remove the kickplate and try turning the motor fan blades by hand with the motor in place. Sometimes the seal just gets a little dried out and sticky.

The pump on these machines can be rebuilt. Your appliance parts dealer a seal kit available. There is also a rebuilt pump and motor unit generally available.

TECH TIPS

These are pretty straightforward machines to disassemble. Unplug the machine. Have a shallow pan standing by to catch any water left in the pump and disconnect all hoses from the pump. Disconnect the motor leads, the motor mount and the pump suction inlet and discharge.

A macerator is located outside the pump screen. This macerator chops up bits of food and debris before it enters the pump. Two different kinds of macerators were used; a blade-type, and a wire-type. If you have a blade-type, hold the motor fan blades and unscrew the macerator from the impeller. If you have a wire-type, there is no need to remove it yet.

There are tabs molded into the suction port nut for removal. Using the flat side of a file to turn the nut, unscrew the suction port nut from the pump body. If you have a metal suction screen, this will be difficult. Loosen it by grabbing the metal suction screen and yanking it out with a pair of needlenose pliers. This will destroy the screen, but it's cheap to replace, and it will loosen the nut. Remove the plastic ring and the metal wear ring. Note how they come out for re-installation.

NOTE: The suction port nut has left-hand threads! Turn it clockwise to remove it!

Hold the motor fan blades and unscrew the impeller. Hold the impeller with a pair of pliers (careful not to damage the threads unless you are replacing it) and turn the motor fan blades.

Remove the pump body from the motor and knock out the pump shaft seal from the outside.

Assembly is the opposite of disassembly. Make sure the lip on the metal wear ring points towards the impeller. Don't forget that the suction valve nut has a left-hand thread; turn counter-clockwise to install.

Feel the action of the flapper valve. If it is sticky or leaking, replace the flapper valve shaft seal.

When you get the pump/motor unit back into place and hooked up, pour a gallon of water into the tub before starting the machine. Do not run the pump dry!!!

GENERAL ELECTRIC / HOTPOINT

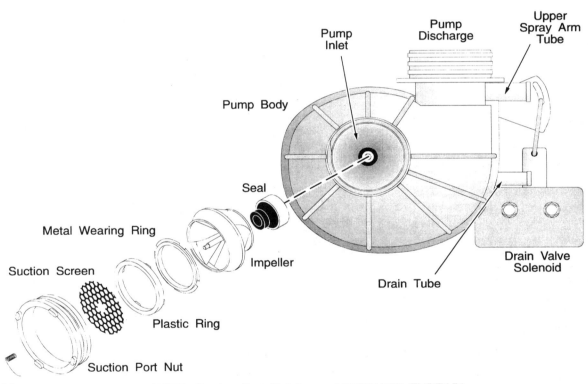

Pump Inlet

Pump Discharge

Upper Spray Arm Tube

Pump Body

Seal

Metal Wearing Ring

Impeller

Suction Screen

Drain Valve Solenoid

Drain Tube

Plastic Ring

Suction Port Nut

Macerator

NOTE: Suction Port Nut has a LEFT-HAND THREAD!
Turn CLOCKWISE to remove,
COUNTER-CLOCKWISE to install.

D&M

TECH NOTES

These are vertical-shaft machines, direct reversing, with two-impellers. Both impellers are used during the wash cycle; the lower impeller feeds the upper spray arm, and vice-versa. During the drain cycle, the motor reverses and the lower impeller pumps out the tub.

Your appliance parts dealer has an impeller and seal kit for these machines.

OLDER MODELS: The pump is disassembled in place, without removing the motor.

Once the pump has been disassembled, the motor can be removed with the machine in place, but it can be a difficult job. The screws are hard to get to. Try it, but if you have too much trouble, pull out the machine.

LATER MODEL: These machines have a split collar on the underside of the tub, atop the motor. The pump and motor can be lifted out as a unit and rebuilt on a bench.

TECH TIPS

These are pretty straightforward machines to tear down and rebuild. Note carefully how everything comes off and in what order.

OLDER MODELS: Unplug the machine and disconnect the motor harness. Have a shallow pan standing by to catch any water left in the pump, and disconnect the drain line. Disassemble the pump as shown in the diagram. Do not remove the lowermost pump housing from the tub. If you have a wet/dry vacuum, you can use it to suck out any water remaining in the pump as you disassemble it. If not, use a turkey baster and sponge or an old towel to remove water.

LATER MODEL: Unplug the machine and disconnect the motor harness. Have a shallow pan standing by to catch any water left in the pump, and disconnect the drain line. Remove the securing screws from inside the tub, then remove the collar and lift the pump and motor out as a unit. You can then rebuild the pump on a bench.

About the only trick to reassembly is that the lower impeller must be shimmed to the proper clearance. This is the impeller with the tall center hub, and it can be difficult to keep the shims in place while you lower the impeller over the shaft. Use a little Vaseline® to stick the shims to the shaft. To shim the impeller to the proper height, a cardboard gauge comes with the impeller kit.

There are two different impeller kits for two different designs. Make sure you get the right one. The new style lower impeller (the one with the shoulder) will work properly in an old machine. But if you put the older impeller into a new machine, it will drain during the wash cycle.

If you are replacing the seals because of a leak, make sure you turn the motor shaft by hand and check the motor for any stickiness or grittiness.

When you get the pump back together and hooked up, pour a gallon of water into the tub before starting the machine. Do not run the pump dry!!!

D & M Machines

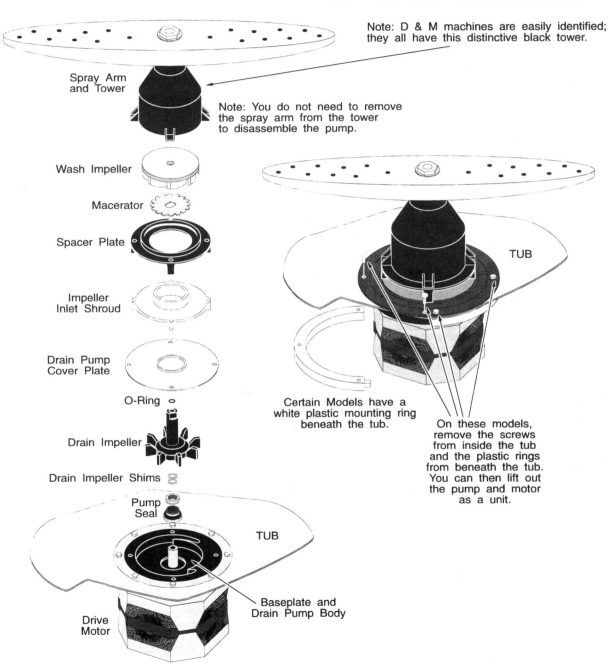

Note: D & M machines are easily identified; they all have this distinctive black tower.

Spray Arm and Tower

Note: You do not need to remove the spray arm from the tower to disassemble the pump.

Wash Impeller

Macerator

Spacer Plate

Impeller Inlet Shroud

Drain Pump Cover Plate

O-Ring

Drain Impeller

Drain Impeller Shims

Pump Seal

TUB

TUB

Certain Models have a white plastic mounting ring beneath the tub.

On these models, remove the screws from inside the tub and the plastic rings from beneath the tub. You can then lift out the pump and motor as a unit.

Baseplate and Drain Pump Body

Drive Motor

MAYTAG

TECH NOTES

These are two-impeller, direct-reversing machines. The upper impeller is for wash, the lower for drain. Most machines have a motor mounted in one corner of the machine, which drives the pump unit through a belt. Late model machines have the motor mounted right under the pump, but the parts are virtually the same.

Both the pump unit and motor can easily be removed without removing the machine.

Usually, when these machines go, either the drive belt wears out or the lower pump bearing is shot. The belt may squeal in either case. If the bearing is bad, usually it will feel very gritty when you turn it by hand.

The pump can be rebuilt, but I do not recommend a novice doing it. The lower impeller, lower bearing and drive pulley are difficult to remove and replace. The whole pump module can be replaced with a new or rebuilt unit. It's not cheap; about 60 to 70 bucks if you can find a rebuilt one, 100 or more for a new one. However, these are well-built machines, and usually they are worth the investment.

TECH TIPS

Unplug the machine and remove the kickplate.

The belt stretches; you can just pop it off by hand.

To remove the pump module, unscrew the tower and remove the spray arms. Then remove the strainer and filter. The pump module mounting screws are accessible. When replacing the module, put a little vegetable oil (VERY little!) around the seal to help it slip into place. Make sure it is centered and seated properly and the mounting screw holes are aligned. Tighten the screws as evenly as possible; i.e. tighten opposite screws in pairs.

When you get the pump/motor unit back into place and hooked up, pour a gallon of water into the tub before starting the machine. Do not run the pump dry!!!

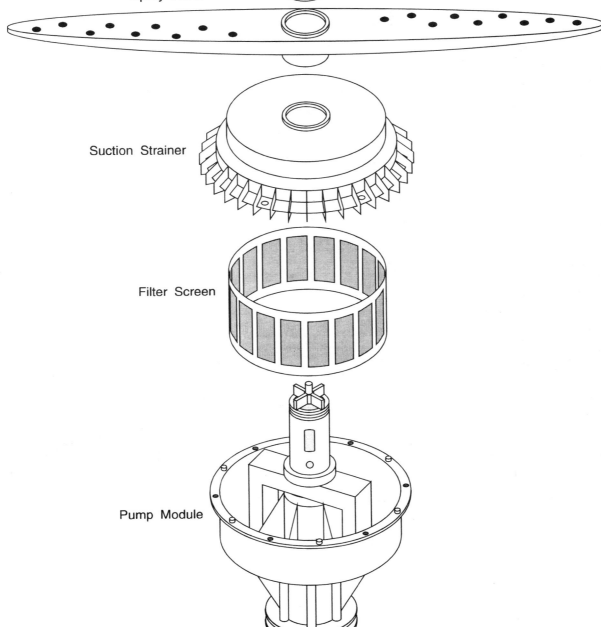

Spray Tower
(unscrew to remove)

Spray Arms

Suction Strainer

Filter Screen

Pump Module

MAYTAG

KITCHENAID

TECH NOTES

These are vertical-shaft, single-direction, two-impeller machines. The upper impeller is for wash, and the lower impeller for drain. A solenoid drain valve opens for the drain cycle. If the machine seems to be draining during the wash cycle, the drain valve may be leaking. Check your diagnosis by opening the air gap during the wash cycle as described in section 3-1.

The pump can be disassembled and rebuilt in place. To remove the motor, you will probably need to remove the machine from beneath the kitchen counter.

Very late-model Kitchenaid machines are built by Whirlpool, and resemble Whirlpool machines in how they come apart. They are direct-reversing, vertical-shaft, two-impeller machines. Compared to the earlier Kitchenaids, their most distinguishing features are two spray arms instead of four, a square-shaped heater instead of round, and Torx-head screws instead of Phillips-head.

TECH TIPS

These are pretty straightforward machines to tear down and rebuild. Note carefully how everything comes off and in what order. The lower spray arms and strainer screen simply lift off.

The impellers are shimmed to the proper clearance. When disassembling, note carefully how many shims are beneath them, and reassemble with the same amount.

When you get the pump back into place and hooked up, pour a gallon of water into the tub before starting the machine. Do not run the pump dry!!!

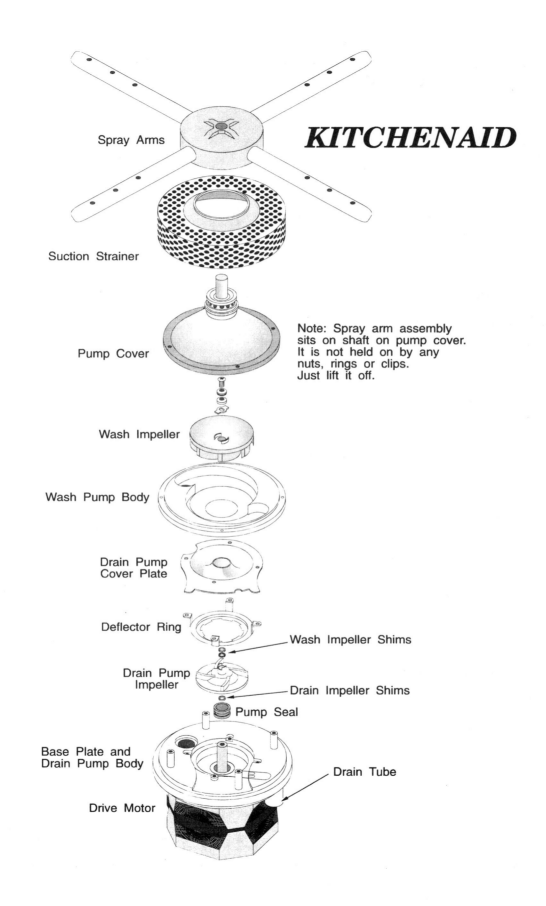

KITCHENAID

Spray Arms

Suction Strainer

Pump Cover

Note: Spray arm assembly sits on shaft on pump cover. It is not held on by any nuts, rings or clips. Just lift it off.

Wash Impeller

Wash Pump Body

Drain Pump Cover Plate

Deflector Ring

Wash Impeller Shims

Drain Pump Impeller

Drain Impeller Shims

Pump Seal

Base Plate and Drain Pump Body

Drain Tube

Drive Motor

WCI/WESTINGHOUSE

TECH NOTES

These are single-direction, horizontal-shaft machines. To change from wash mode to drain mode, a solenoid-operated flapper valve closes off the spray arms and opens the drain port.

You usually need to remove the machine from beneath the countertop to remove the pump and motor unit on these machines.

The pump on these machines CANNOT be rebuilt. It is a sealed unit; you replace the whole pump.

TECH TIPS

Disconnect the motor harness, all hoses, the motor mount and the pump suction inlet. Have a shallow pan standing by to catch any water when you remove the hoses.

Re-assembly is basically the opposite of disassembly. When sliding the motor shaft into the new pump, be careful not to damage the seal. The shaft must be absolutely clean and free of rust, pits or scratches. Go slowly and make sure the shaft is lined up with the impeller.

When you get the pump/motor unit back into place and hooked up, pour a gallon of water into the tub before starting the machine. Do not run the pump dry!!!

WCI / WESTINGHOUSE

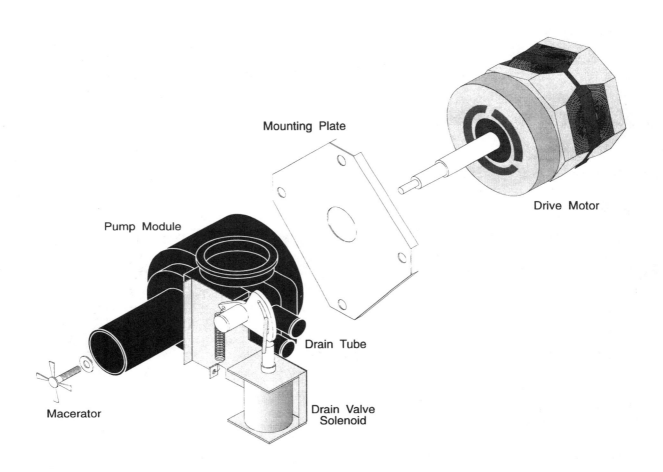

Mounting Plate

Drive Motor

Pump Module

Drain Tube

Macerator

Drain Valve
Solenoid

THERMADOR / WASTE KING

TECH NOTES

These are direct-reversing, vertical-shaft, two-impeller machines.

The pump can be rebuilt, but if the top motor bearing is gone (which it usually is) then you must replace the whole pump/motor unit.

The pump, motor and upper and lower spray arms are removed as a single unit. To get to the motor mounts, you may need to pull the machine out from under the counter.

TECH TIPS

Disconnect power. Disconnect the motor harness. Remove hoses from the pump unit; have a shallow pan standing by to catch any water that may run out.

The pump plate is held in place by clips on the underside of the tub. These are secured by 11/16" nuts. Loosen the nuts, twist the clips out of the way and lift the pump and motor unit out of the tub.

The heater element is mounted directly to the pump housing. The nuts that hold it on are tight as heck and usually cannot be removed without breaking the heater, the pump housing or both. If you are replacing the pump and motor unit and you want to save the old heater, use a pair of diagonals or channelocks and break the pump housing away from the heater. Wear goggles and be careful of bits of flying plastic. Soak the nuts thoroughly in penetrating oil before even *trying* to remove them. Be careful not to twist the heater element or you will ruin it. When re-installing the heater, use new rubber washers.

The same pump unit was used for models *with* heaters and *without* heaters. The new pump unit you get may not be drilled out for the heater, although there should be casting marks where the heater holes are supposed to be. *You* get to drill the holes.

When installing the new unit, be careful to get the pump centered and the rubber gasket seated properly.

When you get the pump/motor unit back into place and hooked up, pour a gallon of water into the tub before starting the machine. Do not run the pump dry!!!

THERMADOR & WASTE KING

Spray Arm Tower

Wash Impeller

Pump Inlet Strainer

Drain Pump Cover Plate

Drain Pump Impeller

Pump Seal

Heater Mounting Holes

Base Plate

Tub Seal

Pump Mounting Nuts and Clips

Remove these to lift pump & motor unit out of the tub

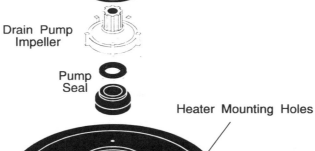
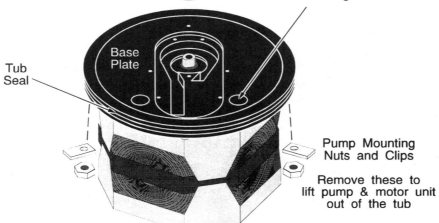

Chapter 6

ELECTRICAL PROBLEMS

Many household handymen will tackle just about any job, but are downright scared of electricity. It's true that you have to be extra careful around live circuits due to the danger of getting shocked. But there's no mystery or voodoo about what we'll be doing. I'll cut out most of the electric theory for you. If you're one of those folks who's a bit timid around electricity, all I can say is read on, and don't be too nervous. It will come to you.

6-1 WIRING DIAGRAM

Sometimes you need to read a wiring diagram, to make sure you are not forgetting to check something. Sometimes you just need to find out what color wire to look for to test a component. It is ESPECIALLY important in diagnosing a bad timer.

Usually your wiring diagram is either pasted to the inside of the door panel, or else contained in a plastic pouch inside the door itself. Either way, you must remove the door panel to get to it as described in section 5-2.

If you already know how to read a wiring diagram, you can skip this section.

Each component should be labelled clearly on your diagram. Look at figure 6-A. The symbols used to represent each component are pretty universal.

Wire colors are abbreviated and shown next to each wire. For example, Y means a yellow wire, V means Violet, R means red, LBU means light blue. Black is usually abbreviated BK, blue is usually BU. GR or GN are green, GY is gray. A wire color with a dash or a slash means - with a - stripe. For example BU-W means Blue with a white stripe, T/R means tan with a red stripe.

A few notes about reading a wiring diagram:

Notice that in some parts of the diagram, the lines are thicker than in other parts. The wiring and switches that are shown as thick lines are inside of the timer.

The small white circles all over the diagram are terminals. These are places where you can disconnect the wire from the component for testing purposes. The small black circles indicate places where one wire is connected to the other. If two wires cross on the diagram without a black dot where they cross, they are not connected.

If you see dotted or shaded lines around a group of wires, this is a switch assembly; for example, a pushbutton selector switch assembly or a relay. It may also be the timer, but whatever it is, it should be clearly marked on the diagram. Any wiring enclosed by a shaded or dotted box is internal to a switch assembly and must be tested as described in section 6-2(a) or (b).

Switches may be numbered or lettered. Usually the terminals on the outside of the timer are stamped or printed with the color of the wire that is supposed to attach to it.

To test a switch with a certain marking, mark and disconnect all the wires. Connect your ohmmeter to the two terminal leads of the switch you want to test. For example, in figure 6-B, if you want to test the door switch, take power off the machine, disconnect the black and tan wires from it and connect one test lead each terminal. Then flick the switch back and forth. It should close and open. If it does, you know that contact inside the switch is good.

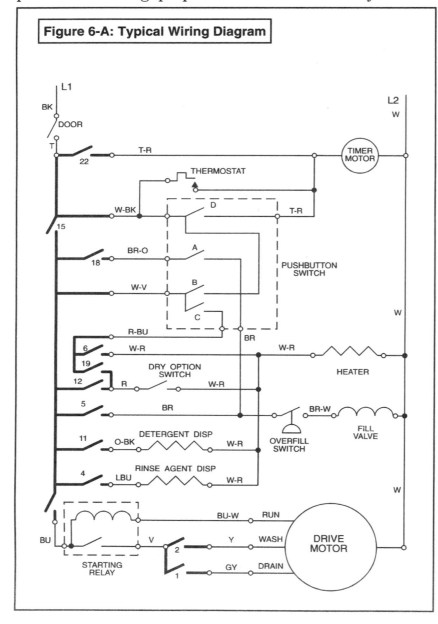

Figure 6-A: Typical Wiring Diagram

Remember that for something to be energized, it must make a complete electrical circuit. You must be able to trace the path that the electricity will take, FROM the wall outlet back TO the wall outlet. This includes not only the component that you suspect, but all switches leading to it, and sometimes other components, too.

In Figure 6-B, which shows a typical electric dishwasher, L1, L2, are the main power leads; they go directly to your wall plug. Between L1 and L2, you will see 110 volts.

Let's say you need to check out why the detergent dispenser is not working.

Following the gray-shaded circuit in figure 6-B, note that the electricity "flows" from L1 to L2.

From L1 the electricity flows to the door switch. The power then goes through a tan wire to the timer. Then it goes through switch number 15, then number 11. These switches are located inside of the timer (you know this because they are drawn with thick lines.) They must be closed.

The electricity then flows through an orange and black wire (O-BK) to the detergent dispenser bimetal. The bimetal is a kind of resistor (the zig-zag lines tell you this.)

Then the electricity flows through a white and red wire to the *heater.* So if the *heater* is burnt out, the *detergent dispenser* won't work. Hmmmm......interesting, huh?

Electricity then flows back to the wall plug, L2, through a white wire.

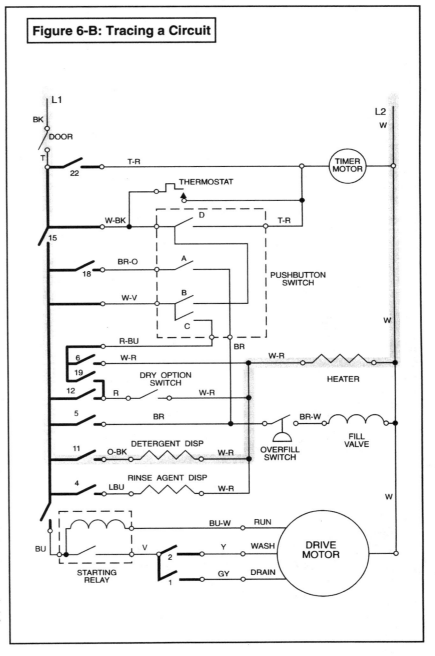

Figure 6-B: Tracing a Circuit

TESTING THE CIRCUIT

To test for the break in the circuit, simply isolate each part of the system (remove the wires from the terminals) and test for continuity. For example, to test the bimetal in our example, pull the wires off each end and test continuity across the terminals as described in section 6-2(f).

Switches 15 and 11 are shown in bold lines, so they are inside the timer. For now, let's ignore them. (The timer is the last thing you should check; see section 6-2(b).

Since a burnt out bimetal element is the most likely cause of this symptom, first test the bimetal for continuity. If you have good continuity, something else in the circuit must be defective. The heater, for example. Test it the same way.

If NONE of the other components appear to be defective, test the timer as described in section 6-2(b).

To check for a wire break, you would pull each end of a wire off the component and test for continuity through the wire. You may need to use jumpers to extend or even bypass the wire; for example, if one end of the wire is in the control console and the other end in underneath the machine. If there is no continuity, there is a break in the wire! It will then be up to you to figure out exactly where that break is-there is no magic way. If you have a broken wire, look along the length of the wire for pinching or chafing. If there is a place where the wires move , check there first. Even if the insulation is O.K., the wire may be broken inside.

Sometimes you can eliminate possibilities just simply be studying the wiring diagram for a few minutes. For example, let's say your timer is not advancing during any cycle. Following the gray line in figure 6-C, the timer is fed through three different circuits. Sometimes it gets its power through timer switch 22, sometimes it gets power from switch "D" inside the pushbutton selector switch, and it can also get power from the thermostat. It is unlikely that all three switches are bad, so the likelihood is that the timer motor itself is on the fritz.

Figure 6-C: Typical Timer Motor Circuit

6-2 TESTING COMPONENTS

Most components are tested simply by removing power and placing a resistance meter across them. However some need to be tested with a volt meter while energized. Occasionally, if the component is inexpensive enough, it's easier to just replace it and see if that solves the problem.

6-2(a) SWITCHES AND SOLENOIDS

Testing switches and solenoids is pretty straightforward. Take all wires off the component and test resistance across it as described in section 2-5(b).

Switches should show good continuity when closed and no continuity when open.

Solenoids should show SOME resistance, but continuity should be good. If a solenoid shows no continuity, there's a broken wire somewhere in the coil. If it shows no resistance at all, it's shorted.

THERMOSTATS

A thermostat is just a switch that opens and closes according to temperature changes that it senses. They can be difficult to test. However, most are usually inexpensive. So if you think you have a bad one, just replace it.

SELECTOR SWITCHBLOCKS

A selector switch block, located in the control panel, is a group of switches all molded into one housing. In your dishwasher, a switchblock will be used to allow you to choose between "normal wash" and "pots and pans" for example, or a "water heat" or "air-dry" option. When you *select* an option, "normal wash," for example, you are *de-selecting* the other options, for example "pots and pans." This is the main function of the switchblock.

Testing switch blocks is much like testing timers. You must look at the wiring diagram to see which of the terminals will be connected when the internal switches are closed.

Keep in mind, however, that you must also know which of the internal switches close when an external button is pressed. When you press one button on the switchblock, several of the switches inside may close at once. To test a switchblock, in addition to the wiring diagram, you must have a chart that gives you this info. Usually this is attached to the wiring diagram or to the timer sequencing chart.

Using the diagram and chart in figure 6-D, let's say we want to test switch "A." We see that with button number 1 pressed, only switches "A" and "D" inside the switchblock are closed. With button number 5 pressed, switches "B" and "D" are closed, and "A" is open. The two wires that connect to switch "A" are the BR-O (brown wire with an orange stripe) and the BR (brown) wire. Remove those two wires and put a resistance meter across those two terminals. Then push buttons 1 and 5 alternately, to see if the switch opens and closes.

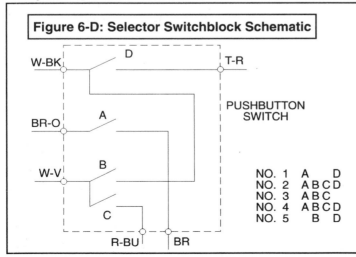

Figure 6-D: Selector Switchblock Schematic

NO. 1	A	D
NO. 2	A B C D	
NO. 3	A B C	
NO. 4	A B C D	
NO. 5	B	D

Test other switches similarly. Figure out when they're closed, when they're open, and test resistance while operating the switch.

If the switchblock is bad, replace it.

6-2(b) TIMERS

The timer is the brain of the dishwasher. It controls everything in the cycle. In addition to telling the motor when to run, it may also activate the heating circuit or heating control circuits, fill valve, detergent dispensers, motor direction or drain valve solenoid, etc.

Most timers are nothing more than a motor that drives a set of cams which open and close switches. Yet it is one of the most expensive parts in your dishwasher, so don't be too quick to diagnose it as the problem. Usually the FIRST thing a layman looks at is the timer; it should be the LAST. And don't forget that timers are electrical parts, which are usually non-returnable. If you buy one, and it turns out not to be the problem, you've just wasted the money.

Solid state timers are difficult and expensive to diagnose. If you suspect a timer problem in a solid-state system, you can try replacing it, but remember that it's expensive and usually non-returnable (being an electrical part.) If you have one of these units that's defective, you can check into the cost of replacing it, but it's been my experience that you usually will end up just replacing the whole dishwasher or calling a technician. If you do call a technician, make sure you ask up front whether they work on solid-state controls.

TIMER DIAGNOSIS

If the timer drive motor is not advancing only in certain cycles, there may be a switch or thermostat that feeds it that is bad. See the example in section 6-1 and figure 6-C.

If the timer is not advancing in all cycles, well, that's pretty obvious. Replace the timer or timer drive motor, or have it rebuilt as described below.

Timers can be difficult to diagnose. The easiest way is to go

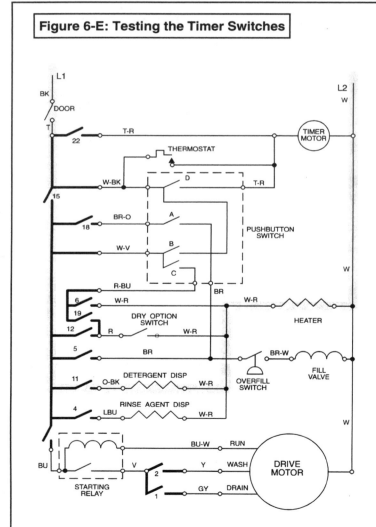

Figure 6-E: Testing the Timer Switches

through everything else in the system that's malfunctioning. If none of the other components are bad, then it may be the timer.

Remember that a timer is simply a set of on-off switches. The switches are turned off and on by a cam, which is driven by the timer motor. Timer wires are color-coded or number-coded.

Let's say you've got a detergent dispenser problem. Following the shaded circuit in figure 6-E, you test the door switch, detergent dispenser and heater. They all test OK. So you think you've traced the problem to your timer.

First take power off the machine or unplug it. Looking at your wiring diagram, you see that the circuit goes through the tan wire entering the timer, and the O-BK wire leaving it. There is also a W-V terminal that you can use to test the switches separately. Remove those wires from the timer. Touch the resistance meter test leads to terminals T and W-V. Make sure the timer is in the "on" position and slowly turn the timer all the way through a full cycle.

You should see continuity make and break at least once in the cycle; usually several times. If it doesn't, the internal contacts are bad; replace the timer. Repeat the process with the test leads between the W-V and the O-BK terminals.

You can drive yourself crazy trying to figure out just exactly when during the cycle the switch is supposed to open and close. Leave that to the design engineers. Just satisfy yourself that the switch is, indeed, opening and closing at some time during the cycle.

In general, timers cannot be rebuilt by the novice. Check with your parts dealer; if it can be rebuilt, he'll get it done for you. If it's a common one, your parts dealer may even have a rebuilt one in stock.

For the most part, if your timer is acting up, you need to replace it. To replace, mark the wires or note the color codes written on the timer. If you need to, you can draw a picture of the terminal arrangement and wire colors. If possible, change over the timer wires one-by-one; it can be easier. If there are any special wiring changes, they will be explained in instructions that come with the new timer.

6-2(c) DRIVE MOTORS AND STARTING RELAY

A motor that is trying to start, but can't for whatever reason, is using one heck of a lot of electricity. If you think about it, essentially the motor is as overloaded as it can be. So much, in fact, that if it is allowed to continue being energized without the shaft turning, it will start burning wires. To prevent this, an overload switch is installed on motors to cut power to them if they don't start within a certain amount of time.

If the motor is trying to start, but can't, you will hear certain things. First will be a click, followed immediately by a buzzing sound. Then, after about 5 to 20 seconds of buzzing, another click and the buzzing will stop. The sounds will keep repeating every minute or two. This is the motor cutting in and out on the overload switch. In some extreme cases, you may even smell burning.

If you hear the motor doing this, but it won't start, disconnect power and disassemble or remove the pump as described in Chapter 5. Check for anything that might be jamming the pump. If so, remove it and you are probably back in business.

See if the pump shaft turns easily by hand. If it feels sticky or gritty, the bearings are probably bad.

Try testing for resistance across the motor windings. In most machines, the white motor lead is common. One at a time, test for resistance between the white lead and the other two or three leads as described in section 2-5(b). There should be *some* resistance. No resistance or no continuity at all indicates a bad motor. Also touch the test leads between each motor lead and the motor cage, or frame. Except for the green lead, there should be no continuity. If there *is* continuity, replace the motor. Continuity between the green motor lead and the motor cage is fine; the green wire is the ground wire.

If you're not sure how to test the motor, take it to your parts dealer or to an electric motor shop. Have them test the motor.

If it won't even start without a load on it, the motor is bad. If you have an ammeter, the stalled motor will be drawing 10 to 20 amps or more. Replace it.

NOTE: When replacing the motor, always use a new relay! They are a matched pair!

STARTING RELAY

Motors use a lot of electricity compared to other electrical components. The switches that control them have to be built bigger than other kinds of switches, with more capacity to carry more electricity.

The switches involved in running an electric motor are too big to conveniently put inside the control console or timer. Besides that, there are safety considerations involved in having you touch a switch that carries that much electricity directly, with your finger.

The way they solve that problem is to make a secondary switch. A big switch that starts the motor, which is closed by the little switch inside the timer or one you push with your finger. A relay.

When you first start a motor, it draws even more power than when it is running. So you need to close a really big switch to start the motor, then open it back up once the motor gets up to speed.

A starting relay is simply an electromagnet that closes the bigger switch. When the motor starts, the electromagnet stops, and the "start" circuit stops. But the "run" circuit stays on, and the motor runs.

Dishwashers have a relay starting switch mounted either beneath the tub or in the control console.

You can usually figure out which terminals to test across by looking at the wiring diagram. If you're not sure how, take the switch to your parts dealer. They can usually help you test the switch. If not, just replace it. They're not too expensive.

If the motor is stalled (buzzing and/or tripping out on the overload switch) and the starting switch tests O.K., the motor is bad. Replace it.

6-2(d) ELECTRIC HEATERS

Electric heater elements are tested by measuring continuity across them as described in section 2-5(b). A good heater will show continuity, but quite a bit of resistance. A bad heater will usually show no continuity at all.

6-2(e) JUNCTION BOX

There is a junction box in either the left front or right front corner of the machine, beneath the kickplate. (See figure 5-C in Chapter 5. The main power leads are attached to the dishwasher inside this box, usually with wire nuts. This connection is subject to vibration and occasionally moisture, and should be considered suspect if the machine isn't getting any power.

6-2(f) DETERGENT DISPENSERS

With one exception, door dispensers are either a solenoid trigger or a bimetallic warp trigger. This trigger touches the spring-loaded dispenser and mechanically pops it open. To test them, remove the wire leads and test resistance across the terminals as described in section 2-5(b).

The exception is GE or Hotpoint machines, in which the dispenser is mechanically tripped by a cam on the timer.

Most solenoids are 110 volt. *BIMETALS ARE NOT!!!* Do NOT put 110 volts across bimetal triggers to test them-you will burn them out. ONLY test them with a resistance meter. They are actually just a form of resistor, so you should see some resistance. If they are fried, you will usually see no continuity at all. Replace the part.

The voltage is cut is by putting the bimetal in series with another component, usually the heater. "In series" means that the electricity must go through both the heater and the bimetal to complete the circuit. When two components are in series, they "share" the full voltage. The higher the

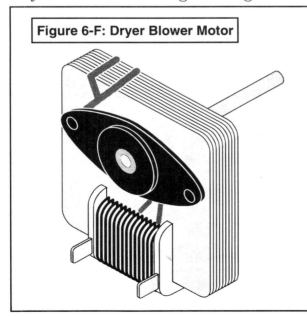

Figure 6-F: Dryer Blower Motor

resistance, relative to the other component, the more voltage it will "steal" from the other component. Since the resistance of the heater is very high compared to the resistance of the bimetal, the heater takes most of the voltage, and the bimetal is left with only a few volts.

Note that certain Kitchenaid and Thermador machines use a similar, but different system. Many of these machines used a solenoid to open the detergent dispenser, but some used a bimetal. On those that used a bimetal, the bimetal is wired in series with the drive motor, and the opening of the detergent dispenser depends on how much current the motor is using. How much current the motor is using depends on the load on the motor. If the load on the motor is too low, it will not draw enough current, and the bimetal will not trigger the dispenser open, even if the bimetal is in good condition. What will cause a low load on the motor? Low water level. *So in Kitchenaid and Thermador machines with bimetal triggers, a* **low water level** *will cause the detergent dispenser not to open!*

If the door dispenser in these machines is not opening, check the water inlet valve for proper operation. Specifically, check that the inlet strainer screen is clear, and if the valve has been replaced recently, make sure you got the right valve, with the right flow control washer. (See section 6-2(h).

6-2(g) BLOWER MOTOR (Figure 6-F)

If your machine uses a blower to dry the dishes, it is located beneath the tub, usually on the right side of the machine. To test, unplug the machine and remove the two motor leads. Test for continuity as described in section 2-5(b). No continuity indicates a break in the winding. There should be *some* resistance.

Also touch the test leads between each motor lead and the motor cage (frame.) There should be no continuity. If there is, replace the motor.

6-2(h) WATER VALVE

The water fill valve (also the drain valve, on older Kitchenaid machines) is solenoid operated. Test them for continuity as described in section 2-5(b) and replace if defective.

When replacing the fill valve, use an O.E.M. part, or at least make sure the flow control washer is the same as in the original machine. Aftermarket parts may have a different flow control washer, which can cause high or low waterfill in your machine.

Index

ABOUT THE AUTHOR

Douglas Emley is Chief Officer in charge of hazardous materials on-board a Merchant Marine ship. He holds a Bachelor of Science degree, engineer's license and officer's license from the Kings Point Merchant Marine Academy, Long Island, New York. Emley has been a major appliance service technician for nearly ten years. Tired of seeing individuals pay his service fees for simple repairs, Emley decided to write easy-to-understand repair guides. "The manufacturers service manuals are too confusing for the average do-it-yourselfer. In my opinion, they contain far too much unnecessary information."

To simplify the diagnosis and repair process, Emley deliberately avoids technical terminology in his instructions. "I'd rather show the average person how to save a fortune by diagnosing the problem themselves and fixing the simple stuff -- 95% of all repairs! When there's a *serious* problem, then call out the tech and pay for his expertise."

No Headache Guide to Home Repair™ Series --

Refrigerator Repair Under $40 -- ISBN 1-884348-00-9
Washing Machine Repair Under $40 -- ISBN 1-884348-02-5
Clothes Dryer Repair Under $40 -- ISBN 1-884348-01-7
Dishwasher Repair Under $40 -- ISBN 1-884348-03-3

These books can be ordered through your local library, bookstore or by mail order. Send check or money order to: New Century Publishing, P.O. Box 9861, Fountain Valley, CA 92708. Each title is $12.95; please include $3.50 shipping/handling (allow 4 weeks for delivery). California residents please add 7.75% sales tax. To order using MasterCard or Visa call (800)392-0907. Volume discounts are available by calling (714)554-2020.